Routledge Revivals

Introduction to the Economic History of China

First published in 1954, *Introduction to the Economic History of China* is a pioneering study of a subject largely unexplored by Western scholarship at the time. Professor Kirby examines key periods in Chinese history, identifying critical issues for further study and evaluating source materials. His analysis offers a vivid portrayal of China's historical development and its broader impact on Asian societies. Notably, Kirby provides a critical assessment of Marxism's global relevance. Drawing on sources from the Far East, the West, and Russia, this original and lucid work remains an indispensable resource for scholars of Chinese economic history.

Introduction to the Economic History of China

E. Stuart Kirby

Routledge
Taylor & Francis Group
ROUTLEDGE REVIVALS

First published in 1954
by George Allen & Unwin Ltd.

This edition first published in 2026 by Routledge
4 Park Square, Milton Park, Abingdon, Oxon, OX14 4RN

and by Routledge
605 Third Avenue, New York, NY 10158

Routledge is an imprint of the Taylor & Francis Group, an informa business

A Library of Congress record exists under LCCN: 54001075

ISBN: 978-1-041-34011-9 (hbk)
ISBN: 978-1-003-79063-1 (ebk)
ISBN: 978-1-041-34013-3 (pbk)

Book DOI 10.4324/9781003790631

INTRODUCTION TO THE ECONOMIC HISTORY OF CHINA

BY E. STUART KIRBY
B.SC. (ECON.), PH.D. (LOND.)
Professor of Economics and Political Science
University of Hongkong

LONDON
GEORGE ALLEN & UNWIN LTD
RUSKIN HOUSE MUSEUM STREET

First published in 1954

Printed in Great Britain
in 11 on 12 point Garamond
by Jarrold and Sons Limited
Norwich

Look up, up, to the mountain peaks:
But keep your feet on the broad high road.

SSU-MA CHIEN

ACKNOWLEDGEMENTS

Studies leading to the preparation of this volume were made possible by a grant from the Rockefeller Foundation for the years 1950 and 1951, covering the expenses directly involved, including travel to Japan in that period. The grant was administered by the University of Hongkong, in which I hold the Chair of Economics and Political Science.

My cordial thanks are due for the understanding and assistance extended by Japanese scholars in the fields concerned, at the many universities and institutions I visited at Tokyo, Kyoto and elsewhere. Their names, and their individual actions in support of my work, are really too numerous for detailed mention. I would wish, however, to refer particularly to the Oriental Research Institute at Tokyo, and the Institute for the Humanities at the (Imperial) University of Kyoto, with their Directors and staffs; together with those at the Hitotsubashi University, Tokyo, who have so liberally concurred in my direct and extensive use of their material published in Japanese.

I am similarly indebted to a number of Chinese scholars—whose names, for quite another reason, I cannot cite at present—who have assisted me by correspondence and by furnishing material, sometimes in defiance of a political regime which classes a study of this sort as 'cultural aggression'.

Personal assistance in research and bibliography has been rendered by Mr. Y. C. Wang, now at Stanford University, and Mr. Alfred Khu of Hongkong, to whom I am especially grateful.

The substance of the present work, in condensed form, appeared as a series of articles in the *Far Eastern Economic Review*, Hongkong, between May 1952 and February 1953. I am grateful to the proprietors of that journal for their free permission to make use of material originally appearing in its pages, which is here presented in an extended and revised form.

None of the above-mentioned persons or institutions is, however, in any way responsible for the views and conclusions in the following pages, which are entirely my own.

HONGKONG, 1953 E. S. K.

CONTENTS

CHAPTER I

PREFACE: THE PROBLEMS AND THE DANGER

The following pages provide an extensive introduction to the study of the Economic History of China, together with a carefully selected bibliography of some 800 books and articles. The text is intended to define, in the first place, the nature and importance of the subject, and to furnish a general guide to its further exploration in future.

Elaborate cross-references and footnotes have been entirely avoided in the text, where full annotation would seriously encumber the reader; bibliographical notes are given by chapters at the end. An adequate subject index is also provided at the end of the book.

The bibliography includes some critical comments, indicating the nature and relative value of different works. While being comprehensive, it is necessarily selective, in the sense of emphasising works which the author has found most helpful from the particular point of view of this study, and those which deserve to be better known to the English-reading public.

This is the first work of its kind. There does not exist, in English or any other European language, any single or satisfactory work specifically on the Economic History of China. There are, of course, numerous monographs dealing with one aspect or one period in the Economic History of China, but practically no work which represents a single or integral treatment of this essential theme. We have, in fair number and varying degrees of adequacy, general, social, cultural and other histories of China, which must necessarily bear on the economic field, and make some incidental contributions to it; but there is none which is specifically and analytically economic, in intention or effect.

This statement is a generalisation, which will be more critically examined below; but it will be widely acceptable as a starting point in this discussion. The lack of such a concretely

'Economic' History of China would in any circumstances be a serious gap in Western scholarship. In the present situation, the deficiency implies something more; it constitutes a definite danger, from the intellectual and political point of view. For China has fallen under a doctrinal regime, one of the basic tenets of which is the attribution of a special importance to economic history, the reduction of all history to its economic aspect, and the projection of the conclusions thus reached into the present and future, as determinants of current practice.

If there exists no unitary or standard Economic History of China in Occidental languages (even Russian), such is naturally not the case in Chinese, in which there is a vast literature with a number of basic works in this field. The 'economic' intention and treatment in Chinese historiography are, however, entirely recent. Apart from some slight and temporary influence of the European (and American) 'Historical School' of Economics and Sociology in the early part of the present century, the rise of economic history as a subject of study in China has been associated very largely with the Marxist currents in that country. It has used the Marxian terminology and methods throughout. From the scientific point of view, these are now 'dated' and difficult of application, even in those Western countries which Marx himself knew.

Marx's views on the subject were crystallised one hundred years ago; meanwhile all the social and technical conditions, and the whole basis of scientific thought, have completely changed. When these views and this terminology were applied to the exotic and heterogeneous conditions of China, the resultant confusion and distortion were very great. The essential terms—even those which are inherently the most simple, and even those which are the least discrepantly used in Russia and other Communist countries—are carried to the extremes of jargon and irrelevance in contemporary China. Such expressions as 'feudal', 'monopoly', 'proletariat', etc., are used so indiscriminately and anachronistically as to rob them of all meaning.

Unless and until there has been a great 'Rectification of Names' in the Chinese academic world, and free and equal discussion is restored between Chinese and Western scholars, there is no possibility of their mutual understanding—they will not even be speaking the same language. The Communist State is vigorously pursuing the opposite policy, however, in both these respects. It has imposed an intellectual blockade of China; all communications are severely discouraged, except in the direction of Russia. Internally, all existing works and opinions are being made to conform to the Sino-Marxist 'line', not only in content, but also in manner and style. All documents or evidences not amenable to this procrustean treatment are being falsified, ignored or suppressed.

Fortunately, a great deal of material exists outside Communist China, which might be used for a reconstruction of this subject, to rescue this field of study from the prospects of Sino-Russian inbreeding and political stultification. Expert work in this field is continuing in Formosa. A great expansion of Sinological studies is proceeding in the United States, extensively equipped and provided; and there is some expansion in Britain, Australia and elsewhere.

But the richest storehouse is Japan. Studies in this field had proceeded, before and during the war, to the point of giving Japanese scholarship a leading position in this respect. Most of the eminent Chinese scholars in the field of economic and social history, including those now in academic and cultural command at Peking, graduated in Japan and developed their special ideas and contributions there. Incidentally, this is a specially important, but so far unexplored, instance of contemporary cultural interchange. In the following, the best and most influential translations of principal works in the language concerned are cited.

Japanese libraries are full of material on China—including all the basic and derivative documentation in Chinese, much of which the Peking regime is now concerned to suppress or subvert, as well as the abundant and effective Sinological literature directly in Japanese. Japan has scholars making full use of this material at the highest expert level, in suitable and fairly well equipped institutions, and their work sustains a multifarious activity of journals and societies in Japan.

In the early stages of the present 'overturn' in China, the hopes of the intelligentsia ran high. The hope was that in this realistic and worldly-wise country, professing a truly popular political and cultural basis, surely the crudities of primitive Marxism could be avoided, together with the rigours and constrictions of political Stalinism. It was hoped that the Marxists, in such an environment, would develop a constructive application of their doctrine to changed circumstances. Would they favour the world, at last, with a precise and detailed sociological analysis of the morphological connections between the 'underlying' production-relations and the 'resultant' ideological and social 'symptoms'? Alas, all such hopes have already been disappointed; the innate fundamentalism of the Marxists has again triumphed, and we are farther back than ever, as we behold the century-old economic judgments, which may or may not have been appropriate to Europe in 1850, and the nineteenth-century sociology of Engels-Morgan, applied compulsorily and indiscriminately to East Asian conditions in which their basic assumptions are irrelevant.

A prolonged, and possibly definitive, estrangement between East and West is imminent on this plane. It is a duty, for the free Western peoples, to meet such a threat. One constructive means of doing so is the extension of all types of Sinological and Oriental studies. In this field, economic history claims a key position; yet it has been comparatively little developed, in its application to Asia, by the Western world.

The present publication is intended to appeal to Western students, in particular, to take up this subject in increasing numbers, and to Western authorities to provide facilities in that direction. It is intended more generally to demonstrate the inherent interest and importance of the subject, and to provide an introductory explanation of the state of work in this field, the nature of the problems arising, and the main requirements outstanding. Chinese and Japanese scholars, to whose understanding and competence in this field no Westerner can ever fully attain, must be asked to overlook defects, and co-operate in this common task.

The author's intention is to proceed eventually to the writing of an Economic History of China, in the form of a single-treatise survey on up-to-date lines, such as he has asserted above to be lacking in the Western languages or the Western manner. The present work covers the first, introductory, stage of that task. Until much more has been done in that direction, the scholar must modestly represent himself (in the Chinese classic phrase), as one who leans against another's door, not yet venturing to enter the inner hall.

CHAPTER II

A FORMATIVE PERIOD IN CHINESE HISTORIOGRAPHY

In China the systematic study of the materials of economic history, on modern lines, began with the political movement of Chinese Nationalism in the years 1925–7. Nationalists were hopeful of achieving, with the aid of Western scientific methods, a fresh understanding and justification of their own country's history and individuality. The political movement of 1925–7 was unsuccessful, from the point of view of the intelligentsia; it left China little, if any, nearer to the progressive state they desired. 'Self-criticism' became the rule and sign of the times in educated circles. Social and economic history and theory were subjects much in vogue. An excellent summary for the Western student, referring particularly to this phase, is Wang Yu-Chuan's article in English in *Pacific Affairs*, 1938 (1).

The pioneer Chinese work, in this aspect of the contemporary Renascence, was however T'ao Hsi-sheng's *Analysis of the History of Chinese Society*, 1929, closely followed by his *Chinese Society and the Chinese Revolution* (2). Another eminent authority soon made his initial appearance; namely, Kuo Mo-jo, with his *Study of Ancient Chinese Society* (3), which continued the attempt to define and distinguish a specifically 'Chinese' type of society. T'ao Hsi-sheng was able, however, in the following year (1931) to proceed to the closer study of a selected formative period, with his *Economic History of the Western Han* (4). All the above works have been translated into Japanese, as indicated in the notes below.

The discussion centering around these principal works and some minor ones during the early 1930's, commonly called the 'Chinese Society Controversy', led to the establishment of the magazine *Shih Huo* in 1934 (5). A close knowledge of the contents of his periodical is compulsory for the advanced student. For the four years of its existence edited by T'ao Hsi-sheng, it led in its field, and exerted a remarkable influence. The contributions are very varied, but the magazine was under Marxist auspices and influence from its inception. The title ('Food and Money', or 'Food and Commodities') is the heading used in all the Twenty-four Dynastic Histories of China for the sections dealing with economic affairs.

Ma Cheng-feng produced a general *Economic History of China* in 1935–7 (6). Other contemporary publications deserving special mention are Lu Chen-Yu's *Chinese Society of the Yin and Chou Periods* (7), Tseng Ch'ien's *Ancient Society in China* (8), and Ch'en Hsiao-chiang's *Investigation of the Society and Economy of the Western Han* (9).

All the work mentioned above is uneven in quality, and the factual basis was as yet comparatively undeveloped. There was much preoccupation with questions of methodology—indeed, to an extent resembling the earlier Methodenstreit in Europe. A more astonishing feature is the evidently strong and extensive influence of the European Historical School; the Chinese writers are elaborately concerned to fit Chinese society into that School's scheme of successive stages of economic development. This tendency had influenced Chinese thought from the earliest phase of modern contact with Europe. A vivid instance is Chen Huan-chung's book in English published by the Columbia University Press in 1914, *The Economic Ideas of Confucius and his School.* This work treats the Confucian system directly in the manner and terminology of the Historical School; but it is an accurate and useful account of its subject, still to be strongly recommended.

Concurrently, however, another influence was evident in the Chinese works of the 1930's; that of the Hegelian and Marxian philosophies of history. Special and technical conceptions of 'Oriental' or 'Asiatic' society, 'Oriental Despotism', 'Stagnation', 'Slave Society', 'Feudalism', etc., are freely used, the Hegelian and post-Hegelian background of which is unfamiliar to modern students in the English-speaking countries. It is desirable that, for the latter, training in Oriental economic history should include some briefing in Hegelianism (10).

Japanese work in this field offers invaluable assistance in the criticism of the Hegelian approach in particular, and the European attitude in general. In this connection special reference should be made to the recent *Guide to the Study of Far*

Eastern Economic History in Japanese by a group of scholars at the Hitotsubashi University (Tokyo University of Commerce) (11), to which the present study is deeply indebted. It is an extremely valuable manual for the student.

Japanese critics, from the 1930's onwards, pointed out that the concept of a distinctive 'Oriental' character, for societies or thought-processes, was meaningless from the point of view of observers actually situated in the 'Far East'. It was a concept only arising in the mind of an external observer, and depended on a preconceived pattern of (European) value-judgments.

Europe's first modern knowledge of China came from the Jesuit missionaries of the eighteenth century. An idealised picture of China was painted by the Physiocrats, and by some of the philosophers and encyclopaedists of the Enlightenment, before the French Revolution. This romantic conception has an important and persisting influence, from Montesquieu onwards. It is reflected in Adam Smith; and systematised, with tremendous power and authority, by Hegel. The nineteenth-century European preoccupation with reason-and-progress and subjective (or individualist) freedom stemmed sweepingly from these antecedents. Hegel and his successors presented 'Oriental' conditions, and the characteristic 'despotism'—pertaining to a stage of 'natural spirituality' in which subject and object were not separated—as antitheses of subjective freedom and Western-style progress.

The Historical schools, and nineteenth-century sociology, absorbed much of the foregoing. It is clearly expressed in another basic work which has had a profound influence in the Far East—Weber's *Confucianism and Taoism* (12). Rosthorn's commentary on this last work, as an explanation of the absence in China of those civic and philosophical conceptions which led in Europe to the development of capitalism, should be read conjointly (13).

The following Japanese works shed further light on this question: S. Goto's *Influence of Chinese Thought on France*, 1933, (14), T. Kobayashi's *Chinese Thought and France*, 1939 (15), K. Moriya's *Hegel and Marx on Oriental Society*, 1937 (16), Y. Shima's *Oriental Society and West-European Thought*, 1941 (17), and H. Aikawa's *Historical Views on Oriental Society* (18).

In the European literature of modern Sinology, the name of Wittfogel is pre-eminent, and it may be first cited here in connection with his article in German, *Hegel on China*, 1931 (19).

The other aspect of the Hegelian heritage (including Marxism) is the conception of an eternal principle of human development moving, in universal and identifiable stages, towards ultimate perfection. The Oriental society was postulated as the first, negative and antithetical stage in this development. Karl Marx deeply committed himself to this conception—most specifically in his *Critique of Political Economy*, 1859 (20), which outlines four stages (or modes of production): Asiatic, ancient, feudal, capitalistic. Japanese critics have ably traced the manner in which this conception 'works backward' from the nineteenth-century European conditions—implicitly assumed to be the norm of human progress—to a quite arbitrary conception of earlier conditions in Asia. European criteria of 'productivity', 'exchange and circulation', 'the basic economic unit', etc., may be historically inappropriate to the antecedent Oriental conditions.

But the essential futility of the Marxist approach, in this connection, is deemed to rest also on its failure to advance beyond the state of scientific knowledge of 1859—or perhaps, with Engels, to Morgan's time. Morgan, in his *Ancient Society*, 1877 (21), dealt essentially with the question of the emergence of the state. Engels, in his *Origin of Private Property, etc.* (22) redefined the stages, on the basis of the materialist interpretation of history, as: primitive communism, slavery, feudalism, capitalism and socialism. Maine, Kovalevsky, and other nineteenth-century contributors were thus not accepted by orthodox Marxism.

Oriental scholars have spent a great deal of time and effort over the question, 'to which of (the first three of) Engels' stages does Marx' "Asiatic mode of production" belong?' This was a main feature of the *Social History Controversy* referred to above which gave the initial impetus to modern studies of the subject in China. For a full account, see *passim* (in Chinese) the *Readers' Magazine*, 1931–3, and (in Japanese) S. Okamoto's articles of 1947 and 1948 (23).

* * *

One of Marx' suggestions proved, however, to be especially fertile. Namely, his mention of closed (isolated or 'self-blockaded') economic systems, and large-scale irrigation measures effected by forced labour, as characteristic of the Asiatic mode of production. A particularly valuable work (in English) is Chi Chao-ting's *Key Economic Areas*, 1935 (24), which effectively analyses Chinese history in relation to water-control policies and activities, and the consequent shift in the 'key economic area' from one part of China to another, at various periods.

The major theoretical development of this point is really due to Wittfogel, who (in *Chinese Economy and Society*, 1931) (25) took irrigation to be a main formative factor, and introduced important distinctions between the earlier 'simple' and the later 'developed' Oriental society—or, in Marxist terms, the sub-structure and the superstructure. His general interpretation of Chinese history was elaborated in the pre-war period in subsequent works (26), all of which were translated into Japanese, and were influential in Japan and China. Some translators comment on the importance of the extensive data furnished, for these studies, by the voluminous *Studies and Travels* of the great German traveller, Richthofen (27), who had a keen eye for the economic aspects.

This topic provided a further stimulus in Japan and China. Particular mention should be made of the relevant works of the year 1935 (in Chinese) of Hsu Chung-shu (28), Weng Wen-hao (29) and Tseng Ch'ien (30), and S. Ogura's contribution (in Japanese) of the year 1947 (31).

The discussion, throughout this formative period, was distorted and sterilised by its atmosphere of Methodenstreit, or mere disputation about rival methods of procedure, the effects of which are still felt. Further advance was to come partly from an improvement in the range and quality of the data available, and partly from improvements in ancillary and contingent sciences, which shed light on the social and economic history of China. The progress in the next period will be reviewed in the following chapter.

NOTES TO CHAPTER II

(For Chinese references, *see* Appendix)

(1) *Pacific Affairs*, XI, 3, 'The Development of Modern Social Science in China'. (Translated into Japanese by Hirano and Usami as 'Shina ni okeru Kwagaku-teki Bunken-shi', in *Shina Shakai no Kwagaku-teki Kenkyu*; Iwanami, Tokyo, 1939.)

(3) Japanese translation by Fujieda Jobu, as *Shina Kodai Shakai-shi* Ron, 1931.

(4) Japanese translation (same title) by Amano Gennosuke, 1940.

(5) Half-yearly volumes (I, January–June 1935).

(6) Two vols., 1935–7. Going up to the later Han period, the first volume was translated into Japanese by Tanaka Sei, as 'Shina Keizai Shi', in *Shina Bunka Taikei*, III, 1941.

(7) Japanese translation by Goto Tomoo, as *Shina Genshi Shakai Shi Ko*, 1937.

(10) A selection of original texts of Hegel which are directly relevant to the present subject is given in *Hegel: Gesellschaft, Staat and Geschichte*, Kroener, Leipzig, 1932. There is a great need for further study of the influence of Hegelianism (directly, and through Marxism) on the Far East.

(11) *Keizaigaku Kenkyu no Shiori*, IV (Toyo Keizai Shi); sections on China, by Professors Masabuchi Tatsuo, Muramatsu Yuji and Nakayama Hachiro.

(12) Max Weber, *Konfuzianismus und Taoismus: gesammelte Aufsätze zur Religionssoziologie: Bd. I.* Translated into Japanese by Hosogaya Kanzaburo, as *Jukyo to Dokyo*, 1940.

(13) Arthur von Rosthorn, 'Religion und Wirtschaft in China', in *Hauptprobleme der Soziologie*, Memorials of Max Weber, II, 1923.

(14) Goto Sueo, *Shina Shiso no Furansu Seizen*, 1933.

(15) Kobayashi Taiichiro, *Shina Shiso to Furansu* (Kyoyo Bunko, 1939).

(16) Moriya Katsumi, 'Toyo Shakai ni Kakawaru Hegeru to Marukusu', in *Ajia-teki Seisan Yoshiki* Ron (*Asian Types of Production*, 1937).

(17) Shima Yasuhiko, *Toyo Shakai to Seio Shiso*, 1941.

(18) Aikawa Haruki, 'Toyo Shakai Kan no Shisoshi-teki Kosatsu', in *Shiso*, nos. 145–7, 1935.

(19) K. A. Wittfogel, 'Hegel über China', in *Unter dem Banner des Marxismus*, Jahrgang V, 1931. Japanese translation by Yokogawa Jiro, 'Hegeru no Shina-ron', in *Shina Keizai-shi Kenkyu*, 1935.

(20) Karl Marx, *Zur Kritik der politischen Oekonomie*, Berlin, 1859, re-edited by Kautsky, 1897. One part only appeared (I. Heft). The best of the several Japanese translations is a recent one by Miyakawa (1948). Japanese scholars also use the early manuscript by Marx, 'Grundriss der Kritik der politischen Oekonomie', translated by Sakada.

(21) L. Morgan, *Ancient Society*, 1877. Japanese translation by Yamamoto Sango, *Kodai Shakai*, 1932.

(22) Friedrich Engels, *Der Ursprung der Familie, des Privateigentums und des Staates*, 1884. Recently translated into Japanese by Nishi Masao as *Kazoku, Shiyu-Zaisan, Kokka no Kigen* (Iwanami, 1949).

(23) Okamoto Saburo, 'Ajia-teki Seisan-yoshiki' ('On Asian types of Production'), in *Choryu*, July 1947; and article with similar title in *Shiso*, 287, May 1948.

(24) Japanese translation by Sano Aizo, 1938.

(25) *Wirtschaft and Gesellschaft Chinas. Versuch der wissenschaftlichen Analyse einer grossen asiatischen Agrargesellschaft* (1. Teil, *Produktivkräfte, Produktions und Zirkulationsprozess*), 1931. Japanese translation by Hirano Yoshitaro, 2 vols., 1933–4.

(26) 'Foundations and stages of Chinese Economic History', in *Zeitschrift für Sozialforschung*, 1935; 'Theorie der orientalischen Gesellschaft', in *ibid.*, 1938 (an English version, *New Light on Chinese Society*, followed in 1938; and a Japanese translation, by Moriya, Hirano and others, *Toyo Shakai no Riron*, in 1939). An article, 'Die Grundlagen der chinesischen Arbeiterbewegung' ('The Basis of the Chinese working-class Movement'), original not known to the present writer, was translated in the Japanese magazine *To-A* (*East Asia*), 1932 (v, 2).

(27) *China: Ergebnisse eigener Reisen* . . . etc. Five vols., 1877–1911, Japanese translations of vol. I, pt. I (China and Central Asia) and vol. III, pt. I (SW. China) in *Shina*, I–IV, 1942–3.

(29) 'An Interpretation of the Historical Development of Ancient Irrigation Works' (*Essays in honour of Mr. Tsai's 60th Birthday*, II, 1935).

(31) Ogura Shohei, 'The Significance of Riparian Works and Irrigation in Ancient Chinese Society', *Kikan Daigaku*, II, 1947.

CHAPTER III

THE DEEP ROOTS OF CHINESE MARXISM

It may be asserted that, in the field of intellectual endeavour, the fate of China was decided—as between Communism and Nationalism—not just recently, but about twenty years ago. It was in the early 1930's that Kuomintang Nationalism failed, in the judgment of educated and active Chinese, to give ideological satisfaction or mental stimulation. From that time, its fall was only deferred by increasing the strictness of its political 'tutelage'; and by the circumstances of the Japanese aggression, which brought about a national rally and some efforts at internal peace. Meanwhile, the opposing, Marxist, party was thoroughly and systematically working, not only to gain organisational control in every political and social field, but also to cultivate the impression that it could supply the intellectual and cultural deficiency, that it could offer a full, satisfactory and progressive explanation of Chinese society and its prospects.

It is precisely the study of this field of Chinese history, into which we are now inquiring, that Chinese Communism used as a chief means to its end, on the intellectual and educational plane. Here it was able to establish its own interpretations and conceptions, almost *in vacuo*, largely by default of effective opposition. The Nationalist Government paid little attention in the early period of the 1930's to historical and theoretical work, even at times when it had the sharpest eyes for 'dangerous thoughts' in present-day or practical matters. Meanwhile Chinese Marxism built itself up, to a large extent, in such domains as archaeology, ethnology, philology and other fields of antiquarian study and research. In this field the left wing secured the active or passive support of a large and increasing portion of the educated middle classes. From these classes were furnished the membership of those student movements, and the like, which are still today the source of the Communist 'cadres', far more than are the 'proletariat' or the peasantry.

Similar use was made of new literary movements—the pai hua cult (of writing in the everyday language) in general, and of such writers as Lu Hsun. The latter is now treated with veneration—though others who played a great part at the time were subsequently 'liquidated'. An outstanding figure was the 'Trotskyist' Chen Tu-hsiu. The Nationalist Government, strict as it was against any ordinary subversive propaganda on the level of popular journalism, street-corner meetings, etc., dealt at first with comparative leniency, or seeming indifference, with these academic and cultural movements. Later (by the end of the 1930's) they became the fiercest centres of rebellion and disruption, and were repressed accordingly. But by that time the Marxist cadres had been widely built up, among the 'petty bourgeois' and 'intelligentsia' classes. And—what may be no less important—in such fields as history and social philosophy, Chinese intellectual life had by that time been deeply and persistently imbued with the underlying Marxist spirit, and thoroughly habituated to Marxist standards of material, treatment and phraseology.

The deeper roots of Chinese Marxism are really here. As one able reporter (1) has rightly stressed, specific agitations (such as land reform, anti-foreignism, etc.) are ephemeral and transitory, compared to the sustained process of 'brain-washing', which means lasting and complete indoctrination. Here we are concerned, however, with a preliminary stage of this process, and with one field of thought which was especially utilised for it—the study of economic history. It was suggested in the previous chapter that the first progress of Marxism, in that field as in others, was partly ascribable to disillusionment, or the default of other doctrines. Most of the present leaders of Marxist thought in China began, it was noted, in the period 1927–33 as exponents of the attempt to distinguish a specifically or characteristically 'Chinese' society and culture; mostly they failed, and in the next decade turned to Marxism. Outstanding examples must be Kuo Mo-jo and T'ao Hsi-sheng, mentioned in that connection in the last chapter. The former is now popularly described as the 'Cultural Premier' of China, and his position has been compared to that of Lunacharsky, Russia's first Commissar for Culture in the early 1920's (though his methods are not the same). A great number of lesser men followed the same evolution, more or less intensely, and to a greater or lesser extent. A very great number of 'fellow travellers' joined them temporarily, usually dropping off after one or more stages of the journey.

It is possible that few movements in China gained a greater number of effective adherents, and likely that none gained so many from among men of superior intellectual ability, as the 'Chinese History Controversy' of the 1930's, calling for a full study and reformulation of the historical 'personality' of the Chinese nation, and its social and cultural identity. This led swiftly to the denial of any 'separateness' or abnormality in the case of China, and the identification of China's recent situation with the earlier stages of Near Eastern and European development. From this it was a short step to clamour for progress towards the later stages, along the scale dogmatically postulated.

Another short step was allegiance (or at least lack of intellectual opposition) to the party which claimed that it alone had a 'scientific' understanding of these predetermined stages, and that it alone had a 'practical' way of reaching them. The whole process is conveniently surveyed in the pages of a Chinese periodical, *The Ancient History Dispute* (2), which spans the whole period in question (vols. 1–7, 1926–41). This was the work of Ku Chieh-kang and his school, who are also responsible for the very useful and stimulating magazine *Tribute of Yu* (half-yearly vols. 1–7, 1934–7). This is an independent source, which, alongside the *Shih Huo*, is a necessity to every specialist in this subject (3).

The following features may be especially remarked.

First the outcome showed the weakness of Nationalistic attempts to identify Chinese civilisation as 'separate' from world-civilisation in general, or as a 'type' of its own. These attempts could in any case appeal only to the more parochially minded elements of the population (e.g. rural landowners) and hardly at all to unprivileged business classes, the struggling peasants, or the urbanised 'proletariat'. In this, the 'united front' of the last three is already foreshadowed.

In the second place, Nationalistic cults departed also from

the profoundly humane and humanistic content of the older Chinese traditions. The Kuomintang increasingly stressed institutions and institutional powers. The climax of this tendency is said to have been reached in Generalissimo Chiang Kai-shek's book *China's Destiny*, 1941, which deals almost entirely in 'power-political' or authoritarian terms; and in the 'New Life' movement, a puritanical and traditionalist cult which seemed a far call from the liberal and cosmopolitan evolutionism of Sun Yat Sen. Humanistic thought, and humanitarian impulses, were diverted to some extent into the oppositionist theories of the class struggle.

A third consideration is that the main need of China was then (as indeed it still is now) the development of business—the opening-up of nation-wide markets and investment and the improvement of foreign trade. The Nationalist regime—and wartime circumstances—blocked and restricted the development of business, traffic and trade in all the middle and lower ranges of commerce and industry, while promoting monopolistic privileges for certain inner coteries of entrepreneur-politicians. This was a very strong, though underlying, factor. It may still be so today, when further thwarting of the business impetus could be just as dangerous to the regime as its diversion to warlike and wasteful purposes. Attention was focused on the institutional and political obstacles to capitalistic development in China, and on the 'defects' of character or temperament which prevented China from attaining such development as Europe had accomplished. The conviction grew that China had every inherent possibility of comparable development, but merely stood belatedly on the lower slopes of the same ascent, the climbing of which was opposed and thwarted by the regime in China, and by foreign interests.

A fourth reason why Chinese thought came under such 'totalitarian' influences, in the second quarter of the twentieth century, is that in the academic sphere German sociological and historical theories appealed particularly, in this situation. They were authoritative in their style of presentation, and comprehensive in their pretentions. These qualities were much more to the Chinese mind, and in line with collective traditions such as their family and clan systems, than liberalism, or pragmatism, or Anglo-Saxon individualism, or French logic, or other available attitudes. Thus Chinese thought grew more and more along the lines of development which may be marked by such names as Weber, Sombart and Marx-Engels.

Finally, from the technical point of view of historical explanation, the Marxist school of thought gained greatly also, because it did play the greatest part in presenting one of the most telling ideas, which probably did more than any other to clarify contemporary understanding of the early history of China. No other school, as it happened, made any such distinctive and useful contribution in this period. The contribution in question is the attribution of special importance to the problems of irrigation. The thesis is that from the social and political points of view, the needs of flood control and the like imposed on China, from the earliest times, a disciplined form of collectivism, with compulsory labour.

From the economic point of view, the argument adds, the availability of irrigation-water, regularity of river-flows, etc., determined which part of China should become, in each successive stage of development, 'the key economic area'; while methods of dealing with the irrigation problem brought about a particular class-structure and particular methods or patterns of exploitation. It is true that this type of analysis owes much to K. A. Wittfogel (who was then in Germany and is now in America); but it was effectively pursued, to more strictly Marxist effect (in the sense indicated in the above lines), by the Far Eastern writers such as Hsu Chung-shu, Weng Wen-hao, Tseng Ch'ien and Ogura, already referred to in the preceding chapter, and by others (4).

The above considerations relate especially to the true norm of typically Chinese thought. They therefore exclude the 'foreign-style' efforts of 'returned students' and others, and also many attempts at compromise or eclecticism. The march of events is swiftly showing how superficial, or extraneous, were the efforts of even the best of these, and how much deeper was the main current which is here chiefly in question. A vivid instance, worth quoting as best known abroad, is possibly that of Lin Yu-tang, whose brilliant and hopeful contribution now appears to 'date' accordingly (*My Country and My People*, 1936).

In his 'dangerous thoughts', this writer was in advance of his times, but in his safe ones he was in retard of them. The wheel (by this period of the 1930's) had turned another full circle, since the days when China and Europe first took notice of each other. A re-reading of Reichwein's classic (*China and Europe*, 1925, from the German edition of 1923) will make this clear at the present day. But, like all wheels that do not revolve in mid-air, it now stood some distance from its starting-point.

Policies and programmes which do not state a clear conception of what China is, and where China stands, in relation to the general perspective of human development all over the world, are empty and ineffective. A mere change of regime is not a sufficient prospectus for the Chinese people, however good the practical programme offered. The question is, in addition, which of the contestants proves himself to have the best claim to interpret and represent China. Both sides at present are weakened by their association with, or dependence on, foreign powers—Russia in the one case, America in the other. But meanwhile the Communist side has worked hard and effectively, over the past quarter of a century, to claim that Chinese history is on its side, and that it represents the real China. In this field it has struck deep roots; the depth and strength of these are still hard to judge, but they must be considerable.

The struggle for China will be won by the party which has mastery over the mind of China, rather than the mere possession of its territory. In this struggle, the understanding of the social and economic history of China is being made to play a most important part.

NOTES TO CHAPTER III

(1) Edward C. Hunter, *Brain Washing in China*, 1951.

(4) See also Wan Kuo-ting, op. cit. Appendix, 1934. Chen Chao-ching, *History of Water-control in China*, 1937. (Japanese translation by Tanabe Shin, in *Shina Bunka Shi Taikei*, 1941.)

CHAPTER IV

THE FOUNDATIONS OF CHINESE HISTORY

Marxism, having secured (as described in the last chapter) quite a strong position in China in the early 1930's, in that field of thought which comprises sociology and social history, proceeded thereafter to extend its influence into various other spheres of intellectual endeavour. This period—the middle 1930's—was that of the Communists' special reliance on the 'United Front' tactic, when they subscribed to every possible group or sect, claiming that they had common cause with all 'progressive' movements.

There were indeed many new and progressive movements in China at that time, which could be utilised for this policy. In a country so long riven with local and factional differences, dissensions and civil war, the call of 'unity' had a strong appeal; often, the instinctive response was too hasty and powerful to allow the hearer much pause for logical or critical reflection. Ready-made answers and easy catchwords had a quick success.

Nevertheless, though some of the support won by the new movement was thus shallow in nature, and even adventitious, it would be unjust and misleading to represent the situation entirely in this light. There did occur a thoroughly honest and well-considered attempt to draw together the results and findings of all the previous work of scholarship, from all the diverse fields of Sinological research and study. It was a cause of grave concern, to serious students, that conclusions from the field of social and general history (for instance) appeared to point in a different direction from those drawn from philology, while archaeology or ethnography seemed to indicate still other conclusions.

Consciousness of the need for a synthesis of the results of work in all the social sciences, and between their separate subjects, and co-ordination of future work on the basis of a community of understanding and purposes between them all, has been the deep and growing conviction of the great majority of sincere Chinese scholars, ever since the beginning of their modern age (i.e. ever since the end of the nineteenth century). By the mid-1930's, this was a general and overwhelming desire. It is for this reason that any closely 'departmentalised' view—treating of one subject at a time—or any 'biographical' procedure, describing Chinese studies writer by writer, can be grossly misleading.

An appropriate instance may be S. Y. Teng's otherwise masterly review of *Chinese Historiography in the Last Fifty Years* (*Far Eastern Quarterly*, February 1949). Excellent and useful as this survey is, it presents the results of the last fifty years, subject by subject, or aspect by aspect (ancient history, general history, literary and artistic history, social and economic history) and period by period. Historians are aptly and accurately identified by their particular interests and inclinations. In the present writer's opinion, this procedure does, however, conceal the important fact that generally they each desired, first and foremost, to 'place' their own subjects or their own points of view in perspective, in relation to all the others, and sought co-ordination, in the sense above described.

* * *

The next field into which the movement flowed, for the expansion of the study of Chinese history, was that of the criticism of the classical literature. Textual criticism was, of course, a matter of long-established practice, from two points of view. One might be described as 'traditionalism', the verification of the authenticity of successive versions, and of successive interpretations and annotations in the innumerable 'commentaries' added by generation after generation of scholars. The other pre-existing point of view was philological, the verification of the meaning, origins and implications of the words, as descended from the classics. Now, in the 1930 period, the new purpose was to relate the old classics to the new-found conception of definite evolutionary stages in history. The first need was to give a precise date to each piece of classical writing; the second to interpret their archaic or allusive language into modern terminology, and the third to explain how each text depicted the conditions and trends of its own period.

There are five classics: *The Book of Changes*, *The Book of History*, *The Book of Poetry*, *The Book of Rites*, and *The Spring and Autumn Annals* (1). These are the Sacred Books of Confucianism. They form a Testament, expounding the biographies, activities, policies and institutions of the god-like 'Holy Kings' and superhuman 'Illustrious Ministers' of extreme antiquity, the sum of which lays down for ever more, in Confucian eyes, the ideal model of thought and conduct for all Chinese, and for any exceptional barbarians who may be able to follow them. This basic Canon is supplemented by the *Four Books*: the *Analects* of Confucius (a record of his aphorisms and *obiter dicta*), *The Great Learning*, the *Doctrine of the Mean* (attributed to Confucius' grandson Tzu-ssu), and the *Book of Mencius* (2).

Moreover, there are many subsidiary sources, variously respected, among which the *Book of Kuan Tzu* should be mentioned first, from the point of view of economic history. It is said to be written by Kuan Chung, an able Prime Minister of the State of Ch'i, who (in the middle of the seventh century B.C.) made that state wealthy and powerful. (It is understood that an English translation is in preparation by Professor F. S. Drake of the University of Hongkong) (3). Others are the *Various Philosophers* of the *Warring-States Period* (480–222 B.C.): Mo Tzu, Lao-Tzu, Hsun-Tzu, Han Fei Tzu, etc. In the Former Han Dynasty, Ssu-Ma Ch'ien (145–85 B.C.) wrote the first 'synthetic' book of Chinese history, the *Historical Records*, assembling the historical contents of all the above Classics, and is the founder of Chinese historiography (4).

The revolutionary and reformist thinkers of the late nineteenth century had effectively criticised the whole classical heritage, from the point of view of philological criticism and the comparative study of various texts, 'old' and 'new'. The 'New Script' School must be particularly mentioned, with the outstanding names of Liu Peng-lu, Kang Yu-wei, Tsui Shih and Tsui Shu (5). This work did not develop greatly in China, on more modern lines, until the 1930's—when it was taken further by Ku Chieh-kang and his school (*see* notes 2, 3 to Chapter III). But in Japan it was meanwhile much developed

—from the point of view of comparing classical texts, not merely with each other, but with the findings of modern science—and later Chinese work owes much to Japanese example. It is in this connection that we first encounter the names of such eminent Japanese historians of China as Shiratori (*Study of Old Chinese Traditions*, 1909, *Higher Criticism of the Historical Canon*, 1921, and *The Origin of Confucianism*, 1912) and Naito (*Methodology of Classical Research*, 1917, *Inquiry into the Historical Canon*, 1921, *Dating of the Tribute of Yu*, 1922, collected together as *Notes on Researches*, 1928) (5).

Ku Chieh-kang's school in China proceeded thereafter to analyse the classical histories, and found them to be the cumulative product of the political disputes and theorisings of the Warring States, Ch'in and Han periods. A good summary of their conclusions is to be found in the Yenching *Annals*, 1928, and in various articles in their publications, *Tribute of Yu* and *The Ancient History Controversy* (6). At the same time, the conclusions of Western scholars such as Chavannes, Pelliot and Maspero, regarding especially the *Tso Commentary*, the *Rites of Chou*, and the *Historical Record*, were gaining wide acceptance and use (7).

In Japan, other methods of scientific verification were also attempted: astronomy was used, to check the calendrical accuracy of the records. The dating of the *Tso Commentary* was especially important, and this point was the subject of much dispute: e.g. T. Ijima (in 1925) asserted it to be a forgery of Liu Hsin of the Former Han, S. Shinjo (in 1928) placed it in the middle of the Warring States period, and S. Tsuda (in 1935) in the Han Dynasty. An early work of Karlgren in Sweden (in 1926) is on the same question, and dates the text (on philological grounds) to the beginning of the Warring States. Subsequent works of Maspero (1932) and Hung Yeh (1937) may be referred to as providing excellent summaries of the general outcome, and also as giving instructive examples of contrasting Oriental and Occidental conclusions (8).

The above may seem to be taking the discussion away from the subject of economic history into purely bibliographical issues. But such is not the case: the question of the dating of the codes of conduct, modes of thought, ways of living and other data revealed by these classic and pseudo-classic source-books, was all-important in tracing the very beginnings of the economic and social history of China. No further progress could be made until views had been developed as to how far the usages and models of society depicted by the classics ever existed, to what period these depictions might relate, and in what order took place the successive modifications which they seemed to reveal.

Equally important, from this point of view, was the task of establishing concordances and chronologies for the main line of Confucian Classicism. The *Rites of Chou* was another particularly important case, which was the subject of further writings by T. Hayashi, Ch'ien Mu, Kuo Mo-jo, Karlgren, etc. (9). The 'Various Philosophers' of the Warring States period also received attention (10). Studies on Kuan Tzu (11), Lord Shang (12) and the Legalists (13) are of special significance for the purposes of economic history.

To a great extent, the results of the body of work just described have not been co-ordinated, and important tasks remain for future students. In the process, however, a great deal of knowledge of the economic events and characteristics of ancient China has been acquired, though it is still incoherently arranged. Oriental scholars, especially, were deliberately concerned, in a marked spirit of iconoclasm, to prove that these Classical Canons were no sacred Revelation from a prehistoric Age of the Gods, but an inspired, and by no means disinterested, political literature from the period of the Warring States. The result of this was inevitably, in the first instance, rather negative; the old canons of historical interpretation were broken down, without any new ones being immediately produced.

The new stress on economic conditions and economic motives was part of the iconoclastic procedure; Marxists, and some other realists, were much concerned to show that much of what had traditionally posed as high idealism and moralism, in fact represented the 'vested interests' of persons and groups, throughout history. Once the abstract principles, and the 'ideology' in general, had thus been rationalised to the satisfaction of the critics, it was time to turn to the task of finding out in detail how people lived in successive periods of Chinese history, and what was the practical mechanism of their social arrangements. But a great deal of ground remained (and still remains) to be cleared, before a definitive science of history, as applied to China, could emerge. Assistance was, however, shortly forthcoming, from such ancillary or contiguous sciences as anthropology, archaeology, ethnology and philology.

The Western student, naturally impatient to advance to later times, expecting to find there the sort of precise documentation and the sort of objective basis for analysis which are available in Europe, is warned that in the case of China he is likely to be frustrated in the former desire, and disappointed in the latter outcome. A great deal of attention has still to be paid to the 'ancient' and 'classical' periods; far more than in the case of any other country, the whole subsequent history of China was set and governed by the classic mould. Right up to the foundation of the Republic, and even beyond, the very form of the documents and arrangements, as well as the general outlook and the underlying philosophy, continued to be those of classical antiquity. The present has never been dissociated with the past, in Chinese thought, at least until recently.

* * *

Prehistoric and antiquarian studies developed very greatly in China, in the decade 1923–33. Thereafter, practical work was greatly disturbed by warfare, but in the next decade much energy was devoted to the digestion of the material previously accumulated. The beginning of the epoch was marked by the sensational discovery, by the Swedish scientist Anderson, of the prehistoric remains known as 'Peking Man'. More important, to the present purpose, are his findings (1923) of pottery and other prehistoric remains, the sites of ancient villages or settlements at Sha Kuo Tun and Yang Shao (14). The 'coloured' earthenware of the latter place was considered to show affinities with previous finds in the Near East and Southern Russia. Anderson held that the Yang Shao people had moved there from the West or South-west. Extensive excavations were conducted in Kansu, and around Sianfu, in 1923 and

1924, resulting in many further finds of coloured potteries; other investigators (Black and Arne) supported the view that this early race in North China had come from the West.

These investigations provided limited, but quite vivid, impressions of the character of the original Chinese society, and its manner of livelihood. It appeared to belong to the New Stone Age, and to have depended mainly on agriculture. The next step was to see how this actual prehistoric society, the first to be discovered, was related to the forms or stages laid down by Chinese classical traditions. Studies of another kind (the interpretation of records found on tortoise-shells and bones, which will be outlined below) at this time suggested that the Yang Shao people might indeed be the legendary Yin Dynasty (traditionally dated 1401–1154 B.C.). Other Yin sites were opened up, after 1928, including the famous Anyang (Siao Tun) and Cheng Tzu Ai (Lung Shan) diggings; and Li Chi and others continued the work of Anderson (15).

A great deal of work was pursued by the Academia Sinica; to summarise somewhat drastically, it may be said that the key problem was that of the relation between three types of pottery which were discovered. There were: first, the 'coloured' wares, found originally by Anderson; second, a dissimilar 'black' earthenware, which is peculiar to China; and third, a 'grey' pottery found in the Yin sites. Liang Ssu-yung (16) considered the Yang Shao coloured wares to be the first in order of antiquity, the black Lung Shan wares to be later, and the grey Siao Tun ones later still. By such criteria as techniques of manufacture, and the shape of the articles, the black and grey potteries are—according to Wu Chin-ting—akin to each other, and are the earliest form of sacrificial vessels in China, while the coloured wares belong to another line altogether (17). The coloured wares were found in the western part of the Yellow Earth plateau, while the black ones were dispersed in the plains to the eastward. H. G. Creel (18) elaborated the hypothesis that the neolithic culture of China consisted of two parts or zones, a Western and an Eastern.

Thus by processes necessarily rough and gradual, but becoming more realistic as time went on, the physical evidences of these primitive cultures were progressively identified with one of the most important of the phases in the formation of the original Chinese society—the Yin civilisation and its replacement by the Chou. The great importance of that ancient epoch, from the point of view of the present study, is that the Chou Dynasty established an original feudal system. In the breakdown of that system, the long vicissitudes of the ensuing Spring and Autumn period, in the era of the Warring States, is found the background for understanding and interpreting the classical culture, and therefore the whole subsequent history of China. Every scholar desired above all things to possess the keys to an understanding of that great age. The Marxists, again, were able quickly and effectively to claim that their keys fitted. The progress of this and other schools, the degree to which a new synthesis emerged from their efforts, the nature of the basic Chinese economy as depicted by them, the accuracy or otherwise of their contentions—all these matters may more comfortably be considered in the next chapter (19).

NOTES TO CHAPTER IV

(5) Tsui Shih, *Studies in the origins of the Historical Records*, 8 vols., 1910.
Tsui Shu, *Records of Textual Criticism*, 1904.

(6) Shiratori Kurakichi, 'Shina Kodensetsu no Kenkyu', Toyo Jiho, CXXXI, 1909; 'Shosho no Koto-hihan', *Toyo Kenkyu* II, 4, 1912; 'Jukyo no Genryu', *To-A no Hikari*, VII, 9, 1912.
Naito Torajiro, *Notes on Researches*, 1928.

(7) Chavannes, *Mémoires Historiques de Se-ma Tsien*, Paris, 5 vols., 1895–1905 (Japanese translation, with a useful introduction, by Iwamura Shinobu, *Shiki Chosaku Ko*, 1939).
Pelliot, 'Le Chou King . . . et le Chang Chou Chen Wen . . .', *Mémoires concernant l'Asie Orientale*, II, 1916.
Maspero, 'Les Légendes mythologiques dans le Chou King', *Journal Asiatique*, II, 1924.

(8) Shinjo Shinzo, *Toyo Tenbungaku Kenkyu*, 1928.
Ijima Tadao, 'Shina Kodai Shi Ron', *Toyo Bunko Ronso*, V, 1929.
Tsuda Sokichi, 'Saden no Shisoshi-teki Kenkyu', *Toyo Bunko Ronso*, XXII, 1935.
Karlgren, 'On the nature and authenticity of the Tso Chuan', *Goteborgs Hogskolas Aarskrift*, XXXII, 1926 (Japanese translation by Ono Shinobu, 'Saden Shingi Ko', 1939); 'The authenticity of the ancient Chinese texts', *Bulletin of Far Eastern Museum*, Stockholm, I, 1929.

Maspero, 'Composition et date du Tso Chuan', *Mélanges Chinois et Bouddhiques*, I, Brussels, 1931–2.

(9) Hayashi Taisuke, in *Shina Kodaishi Kenkyu*, 1927.

(10) Takeuchi Yoshio, *Rongo no Kenkyu*, 1939.
Naito Torajiro, *Roshi no Kenkyu*, 1927; *Ikei Chuyo no Kenkyu*, 1944.
Tsuda Sokichi, 'Dokyo no Shiso to sono Tenkai', *Toyo Bunko So*, VIII, 1927; 'Rongo to Koshi no Shiso', 1946.

(11) 'Revised Views on the Kuan Tzu', in *Rekishigaku Kenkyu*, IV, 6, 1936.
Kimura Eiichi, 'Formation of the Kuan Tzu', in *Shinagaku*, X, special issue, 1942.
Takeuchi Yoshio, 'The Mind and Purpose of Kuan Tzu', *ibid.* (*Shinagaku*, X, 1942).

(13) Kimura Eiichi, *Hoka Shiso no Kenkyu*, 1944.

(14) Anderson, 'Cave Deposit at Sha Kuo Tun in Fengtien', *Palaeontologica Sinica*, D, I, I, 1923; *Children of the Yellow Earth*, London, 1934 (Japanese translation by Matsuzaki Toshikazu, *Kodochi Tai*, 1942); 'Preliminary Report on . . . Kansu . . . with a note by J. D. Black. . . .' *Bulletin of Geological Survey of China*, V, 1925. Arne, 'Painted Stone Age Pottery . . .', *Palaeontologica Sinica*, D, I, 2, 1925. Black, 'Study of . . . Skulls . . .', *ibid.*, D, VI, I, 1928.

(16) In *Birthday Essays for Dr. Tsai Yuen-pei*, II, 1934; 'Report of Anyang Excavations', no. 4, 1936.

(17) Wu Chin-ting, *Prehistoric Pottery in China*, London, 1938.

(18) Creel, *Studies in Early Chinese Culture*, London, 1938; *Birth of China*, N.Y., 1937.

(19) Further bibliography; recent work:
Mizuno Kiyoichi, To-A Kokogaku no Hattatsu, *Kobunka Sokan*, VII, 1948.
Bishop, *Origin of Far Eastern Civilisations*, 1942.
MacNair (ed.), *China* (U.N. Series), 1946. (Goodrich, *Antiquity, to the fall of Shang*.)
Mikami Tsugio, 'Kodai Shina ni okeru Toho to Seiho', in *Kyodo Kenkyu, Kodai Kokka*, 1949.
Kaizuka Shigeki, *Shina Kodai Shigaku no Hattatsu*, 1947.
Sumida Shoichi, *Chukoku Zenshi Bunka*, 1948.
Anderson, 'Researches . . .', *Bulletin of Far Eastern Museum*, Stockholm, XV, 1943.
Bodde, 'Recent Swedish studies', *American Anthropologist*, July–September, 1947.
Sekino Yu, 'Hokushi Zenshi Dogu . . .', in *Shigaku Zasshi*, LVIII, 5, 1949.
Umehara Sueharu, *Shina Kokogaku Ronsetsu*, 1938; *To-A Kokogaku Ronsetsu*, 1944; *To-A no Kodai Bunka*, 1946; *To-A Kokogaku Gaikan*, 1947.
Egami Namio and others, 'Sekai no Rekishi', in *Rekishi no Akebono*, I, 1949.

CHAPTER V

THE PROGRESS OF THOUGHT IN CHINA AND ABROAD

The last chapter described, in summary, the manner in which knowledge of the early history and pre-history of China passed, during the decade of the 1930's, from mythology and surmise to factual evidence and a proved chronology. The effect of the archaeological findings in China may be compared to that achieved, in the case of Europe, by modern investigators, when they first accurately 'placed' the hitherto legendary sites and movements of the Homeric and Hellenic epochs, on a mundane scale of time and place, and related them to preceding and concurrent events in the Eastern Mediterranean. A starting-point was thus given to the scientific treatment of Chinese history. Most important, the actual antecedents and circumstances of that 'model' system of social organisation and thought, the classical society of the supposed Golden Age—the key conception which formed and coloured all subsequent Chinese thought and development—were identified with a specific period, and specific places and personalities (or at least dynasties).

The society thus identified appeared to be merely human in its attributes, not divine; far from representing fixed principles and absolute values, its philosophies were seen to be conflicting, transitory, and in actual process of evolution; its living standards were evidently poor and primitive, especially for the lower classes, while the philosophies put out by the upper classes seemed to be designed to justify their own position and privileges. Marxists and other radicals naturally emphasised these unfavourable evidences; and over the course of years they constantly reiterated the same adverse conclusions.

The effect was iconoclastic in the extreme. Never, perhaps, in the whole history of human culture, has there been so profound and widespread an upsetting of old-established values—unless it were in Russia in the 1920's. This was the seed-time of the present harvest, the significance of which is still not fully appreciated. While the old values and the old images were thus vigorously destroyed, no new ones were provided, at that period, to take their place.

If the Nationalist Government had at that time pursued a more liberal policy and a more enlightened conduct, especially towards academic circles and scholastic affairs, the outcome might have been different. Disillusionment about the past, and the abandonment of traditional codes, might have taken a slower and calmer course; constructive ideas might have had a chance to gain a hearing, and offset the tendency to extremism.

Instead, the ruling party insisted on rather narrow social and political codes. It fashioned thought-controls and secret-police methods like those of European Fascist Governments, and bore with especial severity on academic circles. Some of the student movements were indeed turbulent, but anything of the kind was crudely suppressed, with extreme brutality, and the official interpretation of dangerous thinking was so wide as to include almost any thinking. The atmosphere of this terrorism, and some of the actual persecutions and assassinations, have been well described for Western readers (with vividness, if not with complete accuracy) by Robert Payne.

Economic History was one of the subjects which suffered most from this situation, in view of the special attention given by Marxism to economic factors and economic motives. But in general, no true movement of Reform or Renascence, even under the most honest and enlightened leadership (as, for example, that of Hu Shih) could make much headway in such an environment. Meanwhile the major centres of the country were occupied by the Japanese—who, in their way also, were keen destroyers of all they considered 'dangerous thought'.

Many Chinese patriots put abstract speculation aside, and found other things to do. The Communists had, to a large extent, a clear field. They resisted the persecution; they found time, while preaching resistance against the invader, to continue their studies of class-war, past and present; they secured, at least in appearance, leadership of the national opposition, underground. As thought was driven more and more underground, it passed more and more under the influence of Marxism.

In the next phase, that of the later 1930's, there was a time of false calm (from the point of view of intellectual experimentation) while this influence was being consolidated. While the results of the work outlined in the foregoing were being sifted and absorbed, there was another field in which corroboratory and supplementary evidence was being gathered and assimilated: namely, the field of the interpretation of the varied types of marks and inscriptions on bones, shells and metal articles, dating from the same ancient periods.

If other results from the excavations in China were compared above to those achieved, in the case of Europe, by corresponding work in the Eastern Mediterranean, the results of these studies of inscriptions may perhaps be compared, at least broadly, to those following on the discovery of the Rosetta stone; and students require to be similarly aware of them.

The Shang-Yin people were greatly addicted to magical divination; 'fortunes' were told, or rather the oracles were consulted as to matters of state importance, by subjecting bones of animals, or the shells of tortoises, to the heat of a fire. The resulting cracks were 'read' or interpreted by the wizards (shamans) to give the oracular verdict. Among the bones, the shoulder-blades of sheep were especially used; hence the practice may be referred to as 'scapulimancy'.

Meanwhile, the first and original picture-writing of the Chinese was evolved; and the Chou people produced very fine bronzes, particularly in the form of vessels (like vases, cauldrons, etc.) used for ceremonial sacrifices, on which important affairs were recorded in writing. In all subsequent periods, 'finds' of these relics, of each kind, were made and commented on by scholars and others.

The study of shells and bones was greatly developed in the nineteenth century in China, by the scholars of the so-called 'Lesser Learning'; notably by Lo Chen-yu and Wang Kuo-wei (1). In his *Dukes and Kings in the Yin Oracles*, 1927, the latter was able to show that the names of rulers and lords, and other details in the divination-relics, corresponded very exactly with those given by Ssu-Ma Chien in his *Historical Records* (2). A disciple of Wang Kuo-wei, Tung Tso-pin, carried the procedure still further; it is considered that he was able to date a number of the oracle bones and shells with exactitude, and that he established the historicity of the Yin Dynasty, from its middle period onwards. A very full account is given by Tung Tso-pin, and by Kaizuka in Japan (3) of the progress of this work, and of the general conclusions drawn from it.

Those scientific investigators, who approached the evidence without preconceived ideas about the nature of social development, drew objective conclusions grounded on logic and common sense. But a large number carried into this subject a habit of formalism, taken especially from the types of German sociology which insist on the exact demarcation of topics or stages in the analysis. Their concern was to define exactly to which stage, in a preconceived or conventional series of stages in communal development, a particular fragment belonged. In this connection the name of Kuo Mo-jo must be prominently mentioned. The present 'cultural leader' of Communist China achieved prominence in this field in 1933, with his 'Oracular Terminology'. This gives the classified interpretation of bone and shell markings; but unlike other dictionaries, glossaries or manuals of the sort (4), it classifies them not only according to the name, the place, etc., but also by the 'type of economy' or the 'socio-economic' environment disclosed.

The inscriptions on the Chou bronzes are, broadly speaking, in the nature of epitaphs and ceremonious inscriptions on altar vessels, musical instruments, etc. The study and interpretation of these began in the Sung Dynasty. Like the study of bones and shells, it progressed rapidly in the latter part of the Manchu era. The results for this period were definitively collected by Wu Ta-cheng in 1911. The work was continued, in the Republican era, by Wang Kuo-wei in the 1920's, Wu Chi-chang, Karlgren, Yung Ken and Kuo Mo-jo in the 1930's (5). This afforded a great deal of reliable data from the chronological point of view, relating especially to the earlier or Western Chou, on which there had previously been only the fragmentary indications afforded by the Tso Chuan, the Book of Poetry, the Kuo Yu, etc. Yung Ken's illustrated *Bibliography*, 1936, and his later work form an excellent compendium of the results to that stage. But the Japanese scholar Kaizuka Shigeki has more recently developed the subject very much further (6).

The same remarks apply, in this field, as were made above concerning the study of the oracle bones and shells; there was an academic struggle between those who interpreted these matters with an open mind, in the light of straightforward inference, and those who were concerned, in a spirit of formalism, to reduce the results to an arbitrary and predetermined pattern laid down in their own minds, deriving from the precedents of German sociology or the prescriptions of Marxist manuals.

In China, the latter group prevailed. Even in the pre-war days, they were the more influential. Many Marxists and fellow travellers developed this field of study; one reason was that it was less subject than others to the attentions of the political police and other wardens of Kuomintang orthodoxy. The authorities seemed generally to have been of the view—once expressed by an official to the present writer—that 'messing about with scraps from old graveyards, and museum pieces' could have no relation to 'present politics'. In the difficult task of attempting a new synthesis or systematisation of the amount of new knowledge made available by the generation of workers here cited, many took the easy road of accepting the ready-made formulae which were thus offered; comparatively few, in China, were able to undertake the onerous task of rebuilding and recasting from the very beginning.

In Japan also, Marxism was influential, and became increasingly so. It was, however, always less orthodox than in China, less exclusively associated with the Communist Party and its discipline. A considerable number of Japanese scholars were able to dabble in Marxism, without becoming enmeshed in the wheels of daily politics. As in Europe, 'Reformist' Marxism was able to hold a place in Japan, as a more or less liberal and would-be democratic approach. The actual Communist party organisation, on which the process of mental enslavement depends, was much more efficiently suppressed by the authorities than was the case in China. The authorities, or rather the militaristic and ultra-nationalistic factions which then controlled or influenced them, were able further to steal important weapons from the Communists' own armoury. They were well advanced in the arts of 'brain washing', in securing public recantations by former Communists, etc.

Moreover, they themselves adopted many of the ideas and formulations—or at least the terminology—of Marxism. Just as Hitler's movement in Germany, in its rising phase especially, stressed that it was 'Socialist' as well as 'National', the Japan right wing claimed to stand for the 'proletariat' against 'international capitalism'. It cultivated a mixed terminology, along with a mixture of ideas, drawn from such movements as syndicalism, as well as from purely Japanese traditions and from its European associates. Appreciation of this paradoxical situation is essential, for an understanding of the contemporary evolution of ideas, and of modes of expressing those ideas, in the Far East.

In the Japanese case, moreover, the wartime circumstances worked to increase the independence and self-confidence of liberal-minded and progressive Japanese Sinologists. The Japanese authorities respected their expert status, and evinced a genuine desire to have sound 'background' knowledge of Chinese and Asian affairs, including historical knowledge. Many of the best Japanese scholars were well able to continue their China studies throughout the war, under remarkably free conditions. Bibliographical references in the following will illustrate how abundant and continuous was their output in those years. In this relative freedom, Marxist ideas took far less hold than in China, though certainly the jargon is much practised in the island country also.

Thus, in the realm of Chinese ancient history, the situation in China is that of the unqualified dominance of the attitude and method of Kuo Mo-jo. The work of that scholar has throughout shown various merits. But—starting with a marked xenophobia, which certainly did not diminish in his later career—he moved more and more towards such narrowness of outlook and dogmatism of conclusions as can only be endurable to a thorough Marxist. Wang Kuo-wei drew attention to the differences in social systems between the Yin and Chou dynasties (7). He broadly considered the circumstances of each, and drew cautious conclusions about the nature of the transition from the one system to the other, from the evident fact that a conflict between two races was involved—with broad clashes, but also considerable interpenetration, between them. He showed that the system of primogeniture prevailed among the Chou, and was imposed by them as the basis of their feudal system. The feudal system was thus the outcome of conquest and racial dominance.

But Kuo Mo-jo subjected the whole question to the schematic formulae of Engels-Morgan, laying down that the story of the pre-Ch'in culture of China was that of a clear and inevitable development from a clan system (of relations of consanguinity) to a class system (of economic relationships), the latter exactly exemplifying the primitive 'slave system' imagined by Engels, after Morgan, in the 1880's. Despite the range of his erudition, after years of the assiduous collection of details, his whole interpretation is as mechanistic as it is one-sided.

In this particular field, the dominant school of China ignores or rejects the whole subsequent progress of thought in Europe in the last seventy years, to an extent that is not generally realised. It ignores or despises the devastating criticism applied to Morgan's evolutionist conception of anthropology, which has rejected its evolutionist basis ('the law of survival') as well as its arbitrary framework of stages. Diffusionist theories, 'organic' interpretations, alternative schemes advanced by the German Historical School, Thurnwald's theory of 'layer formation'—these in particular offered a wide range of useful alternative methods and hypothesis. They were ably taken up, in Japan as elsewhere. But in China, these results from ethnology and social anthropology have been broadly rejected, with the victory, in an internal struggle, of a certain type of economic determinism.

In Japan, meanwhile, great progress had been made in every type of Sinological study (8), with a wide and active discussion of differing opinions. Moreover, Japanese scholarship was fully aware of the no less important progress being made at the same time in Sinological studies in the Occident (9), and was as receptive as ever to the influence of foreign ideas.

The negative results, in China itself, of the closure of minds on the ethnological and anthropological aspects, have to some extent been balanced and compensated by a shrewd and active development of investigation and analysis on the lines of the 'water-control' thesis. As noted above, interesting and fruitful contributions were made by Marxist and near-Marxist students, through their consideration of the special importance of 'hydrology' or irrigation in Chinese history. Of this line of work the most convenient instance, for Western readers, is Chao-Ting Chi's *Key Economic Areas in Chinese History, as revealed in the development of public works for Water control*, London, 1936 (10). But this type of interpretation was itself due mainly to Western thought, deriving from European Marxists and others of recent generations, then through Wittfogel in particular, and was effectively carried on in Europe and America as well as (or better than) in China.

Hence it may be asserted that the time is ripe for a complete reassessment and reformulation of the approach to Chinese history, and its basic data; but this cannot be achieved by China, if that country turns its back on the current work being done in Western countries and in Japan, where this new advance in Oriental studies is now gathering speed.

Meanwhile 'cultural' relics and other data are being rapidly exported from China to stock the museums and institutions of the Soviet Union proper, at which the Russians are constantly reporting their pleasure. It remains to be seen whether the Russians will make better use of the material, from the scientific point of view, or a use more friendly to China, than did the 'reactionary', 'superstitious' and 'cannibalistic' West, in the days when it had less access than the Russians now have, for its alleged acts of 'cultural aggression'.

The actual nature of the recent reformulations, and attempts at a new synthesis, effected in the West and in Japan, will be outlined in the next chapter, in which we shall be able, after only a little more of this theoretical ground-clearing, to embark on the actual record of Chinese history.

NOTES TO CHAPTER V

(3) *Academia Sinica*, IV, 1937 (*Symposium for Dr. Tsai's 65th Birthday*); *Academia Sinica*, VI, 3, 1936.
Kaizuka Shigeki, 'New Development of the Study of Shells and Bones', in *Chukoku Kodai Shigaku no Hattatsu*, 1946.

(4) 'Relations between Yin and Chou', in *Yu Kung*, I, 6, 1934.

(5) Karlgren, 'Yin and Chou in Chinese Bronzes', *Bulletin of Museum of Far Eastern Antiquities*, Stockholm, 1930.
(6) Kaizuka, see (3) above.
(7) Wang Kuo-wei, see (2) above.
Hsu Chung-shu, 'The Yin and Chou Peoples from Ancient Texts', in Tsing Hua series, I, 1, 1927.
Fu Ssu-nien, *A.S.*, I, 1, 1930; *ibid.*, 'Report on Anyang Excavation, No. 2', 1930; 'Studies in Yin and Chou cultures', *A.S.*, II, 2, 1932; 'Major and Minor Eastward Movements', *A.S.*, II, 1, 1932; 'The Five Titular Ranks', *A.S.*, II, 1, 1932; 'Chou's Eastern Domain and the Remnants of the Yin', *A.S.*, IV, 3, 1934; 'Eastern and Western Barbarians', in *Essays for the 60th Birthday of Dr. Tsai*, 1935; 'Explanation of certain terms . . .', *A.S.*, V, 1940.
Hu Shih, *A.S.*, IV, 3, 1934. Ch'en Meng-chia, *Yenching Bulletin*, XIX, 1934.
Yang K'uan, *Introduction to the Ancient History of China*, 1941.

HISTORIOGRAPHY

(8) Katsura Isoro, *Kanseki Jisho*, 1905; *Shiseki Kaidan*, 1936 (Heibonsha).
Nagazawa Noriya, *Shinagaku Nyumon*, 1940.
Iwamura Shinobu (ed.), *Obei Meisha no Chukokushi Kenkyu no Bunken Mokuroku*, 1940 (*List of Famous Sinological Books of Europe and America*): virtually a summary of R. J. Kerner's *North-eastern Asia—a selected Bibliography*, Berkeley, 1939.
Social and Economic History Association of Japan (ed.), *Development of the study of Social and Economic History* (*Shakai Keizai Shigaku no Hattatsu*), 1941.
Komatsu and Takamura, *Development of the Study of Economic History in Japan* (*Nihon ni okeru Keizai Shigaku no Hattatsu*), 1949.
Masabuchi Tatsuo, 'Modern Scientific Trends in the Field of Chinese History', in *Hitotsubashi Ronso*, XVII, 3, 4, 1947.
Mori Shikazo, 'Latest Tendencies in Chinese Studies', in *Toko*, II, 3, 1948.
Ishihama Juntaro, 'Oriental Studies in America' ('Amerika no Toyogaku'), in *Toyoshi Kenkyu*, IX, 5–6, 1946; 'Oriental Studies in Russia' ('Toyogaku no Hanashi'), 1943.
Okamoto Saburo, 'Asian Studies in Soviet Russia', in *Rekishigaku*, CXXII, 1946.
Kaizuka Shigeki, *The Expansion of Studies on Chinese Ancient History* (*Shina Kodai Shigaku no Hatten*), 1946.
Naito Torajiro, *History of Chinese Historiography* (*Chukoku Shigaku Shi*), 1949. (A posthumous publication of Prof. Naito's lectures of previous years; this is one of the best books yet available.)

GENERAL HISTORIES

Okazaki Fumio, *Shina Shi Gaisetsu*, 1935. Okazaki (d. 1950) may be considered as the best disciple of Naito Torajiro (see above). His books are difficult to understand, but worth the effort.

Wada Kiyoshi, *Shina*, 1934. Completely revised, as *Shina Shi Gaisetsu*, 1950. This is probably the best general history of China in Japanese.
Miyazaki Ichisada, *Primitivism and Enlightenment (Toyo ni okeru Soboku-shugi no Minzoku to Bunmei-shugi no Shakai)*, 1941; *Ajia Shi Gaisetsu*, 1947; *Toyo-teki Sekai*, 1950.
Ogawa Takuji and Utsunomiya Kiyokichi, *Shina Seiji-Shi* (Hakuyo-sha, *Shina Rekishi Chiri Taikei*, IV, 5), 1941.
Ichimura Sanjiro, *Toyo Shi To (Sequence of Far Eastern History)*, 3 vols., 1939 *seq.*
Niida Noboru and Nohara Shiro, *Sekai no Rekishi* (3) *Toyo*, 1949.

(9) L. C. Goodrich and H. C. Fern, *A Syllabus of the History of Chinese Civilisation and Culture*, N.Y., 1929, rev. ed., 1947.
H. F. MacNair (ed.), *China*, Berkeley, University of California Press, 1946. (U.N. Series.)
C. S. Gardner, *Chinese traditional historiography*, Cambridge, Mass., 1938.
C. S. Gardner, *Union list of selected western books on China in American libraries*, 2nd rev. ed., Washington D.C., 1938.
P. E. Skachkov, *Bibliografia Kitaya; sistematicheskii ukazatel knig i jurnal'nykh statii o Kitae na Russkom yazyke 1730–1930*, Leningrad, 1932.
W. Barthold, *Die geographische und historische Erforschung des Orients mit besonderer Berücksichtigung der russischen Arbeiten, aus dem Russischen übersetzt v. Dr. E. Ramberg-Figulla*, Leipzig, 1913. Translated by Japanese Foreign Office, 1941, as *Oshu ni okeru Toyo Kenkyu Shi.*
S. Y. Teng, 'Chinese historiography in the last fifty years', *Far Eastern Quarterly*, February 1949.
A. Wright, 'Sinology in Peiping 1941–5', *Harvard Journal for Asiatic Studies*, February 1947.
H. Maspero, *Chine et Asie Centrale*, Paris, 1927.
Demiéville, *La Sinologie* (La science française), 1934. Japanese translation by Nohara Shiro, in *Rekishigaku Kenkyu*, III, 2, 1934.
O. Franke, *Die sinologischen Studien in Deutschland*, Hamburg, 1911.
W. Franke, 'The younger generation of German sinologists', *Monumenta Serica*, V, 1940.
J. L. Duyvendak, 'Early Chinese studies in Holland', *T'oung Pao*, 1936.
L. C. Goodrich, 'Chinese Studies in the United States', *The Chinese Social and Political Science Review*, XV, 1931.
M. Cameron, 'Far Eastern Studies in the United States', *Far Eastern Quarterly*, February 1948.
R. Lowenthal, 'Works on the Far East and Central Asia in the U.S.S.R., 1937–47', *Far Eastern Quarterly*, February 1948.
O. Lattimore, 'A Soviet analysis of Chinese Civilisation,' *Pacific Affairs*, XVII, 1, 1944.

(10) See Chapter II, note 24.

CHAPTER VI

THE FIRST DYNASTIES

For reasons shown in the foregoing chapters, the study of Chinese social and economic history was, by the time of the outbreak of the Second World War, in a position to advance to the 'new synthesis' which had so long been desired. This was possible on the international plane at any rate, but in China itself the outlook was more negative; in that country a state of war prevailed, and the most active influences were Marxism and other kinds of formalism.

There were—and still are—three convergent lines of progress on which good expectations were based. The first is continued progress in the accumulation of ethnographical data and the refinement of ethnological conclusions, shedding light on the origin and development of the Chinese people. This traces the infusion, all through history, of other races and elements, and shows ever more clearly the results in terms of the exchange and interpenetration of social and cultural ideas and institutions.

The second is the elaboration and deepening of cyclical interpretations of history, and their application to the case of China. This technique of analysis traces ever more clearly the recurrent process whereby dynasties, systems, or epochs rise, flourish, decline and fall, in seemingly inevitable succession.

The third is the realistic application of findings and conclusions drawing especially on the domain of economic geography. Students in this line of thought are concerned with the physical environment, and the constant struggle of the Chinese people and state against that environment, for their survival, as the main and direct explanation of the nature and course of Chinese history. For what may be called technical reasons, the most important school in this group is that which especially considers 'water-control' or irrigation, as a determinant both of the forms of social and political organisation and of the successive changes in 'key economic areas', in terms of which Chinese history is charted and explained.

An illustrious exponent of recent progress, drawing synthetically on all these trends, is Professor K. A. Wittfogel. Some of his works have been cited above (1), and others may now be mentioned in passing (2). But of special, and possibly epoch-making, significance is his recent *History of Chinese Society: Liao* (3), planned as the first of a series of 'dynastic' volumes, comprehensively reviewing the nature of each successive stage of Chinese social history, in the perspective of its dynamic development.

The great scheme, of which this is the first product, rests partly on the technique of geographical-economic or environmental analysis, mentioned above as the third of the current lines of advance. Equally, however, it rests on the recent achievements of social or cultural anthropology, as developed in America particularly—the explanation of cultural contact leading to cultural transformation, in terms of the definition of 'culture areas' or 'groups' acting upon each other in a process of 'acculturation'. This is included in the first heading above, the progress of ethnology.

The 'cyclical' conception or interpretation is no less distinctly involved, in so far as it is a question of the rise and fall, advance and retreat, of the various alien cultures which successively conquered, dominated or influenced China proper. Absorbing the Chinese culture or being absorbed by it, each in turn left its mark, and was marked by, the process of 'Sinification'. Thus Wittfogel broadly distinguishes two recurrent and interdependent types of Chinese society; the society of the typical Chinese dynasty, metropolitan and socially indigenous to China proper; and the society of the Conquering dynasty, of the races successively conquering and invading from the North, 'barbarian' in origin and usages. He broadly denies the usually accepted idea of 'assimilation' of the latter by the former.

A contributor belonging especially to the first school mentioned (the ethnological conception) came also from Germany; namely, Professor Wolfram Eberhard. His earlier and larger work (in German) *Researches on the Structure of Chinese Culture*, 1942, refers directly to the considerations in question, as is shown by the very subtitles of its parts: vol. I, *Culture and*

Migrations of the Border-peoples of China; vol. II, *Local Cultures in Old China: 1. Cultures of the North and West; 2. Cultures of the North and East* (4). An excellent general summary of his views, a very bold characterisation of the broad perspective of Chinese history, which has been much admired, is his more recent *History of China* (5).

Eberhard appears to have drawn much information from Japanese sources, or to take a position very close to that of some Japanese writers. But his general approach may be inspired, *inter alia*, by the work of Thurnwald (6), who advocated the method of (first) the identification of the significant local cultures and then (second) the study of their successive influence on each other, 'layer upon layer'. Thus Eberhard considers the basic, pre-Ch'in society and economy of China as 'built up' and 'crystallising' gradually through the connection and combination of local groups, different in their character and origin. With this basic principle, orthodox Marxism will have little to do, insisting that all history is the history of class struggles, moving in essentially the same ways, to essentially the same outcome, in all human societies everywhere, from the beginning of history.

Representing the 'water-control' school, or the third line of development noted above, the work of Chi Ch'ao-ting is widely known. For the period of the first formation of Chinese society, up to the unification under the Ch'in and then the Han, he identifies the basins of the Wei, Ching, Fen and Yellow Rivers as the 'key economic area', the consolidation and growth of which determined the process of unification. In constant interaction with the surrounding 'marginal' zones—the complicated zone to the north based on both nomadic and agricultural ways of life, and the great 'barbarian' districts to the east and south, wild areas of swamp and mountain, considered to be the abode of magic—the area of the four northern-central rivers remained according to this thesis, the key economic area, or centre of gravity, of China's development.

It is represented as retaining this preponderant position, and continuing to be the 'key' area, for many centuries; until there came a movement to the southward, which shifted the key economic area to the Kiangnan, i.e. south of the (Yangtse) river and to its lower reaches. There was also, however, in his view, a subsidiary area which frequently exerted an important influence in addition—the fertile and relatively self-contained area of the Szechuan basin in West China (7). A broader view of these peripheral race relations, though representing fundamentally a similar approach, has been ably presented by the Lattimores (8).

All this work—Western, scientific and objective in its method and spirit—must be combined with the results of the very large amount of positive 'study of the classics', the innumerable 'commentaries', produced in China from as early as the Han era (though of course with special attention to modern work from the Manchu period onwards) (9). Unless and until that is done, an adequate understanding of Chinese history will not be attained in either the West or the East. One of the strong points of Japanese scholarship is that it is well able to cover both the one and the other—rather better than Chinese scholarship has so far done, and much better than the West can do (10).

The immense literature of traditional Chinese historiography can only gradually be digested, from the point of view of assimilation to modern and positive standards of textual criticism and analysis. Meanwhile a difficult middle path has to be pursued, between an over-critical attitude which would prevent due use being made of this remarkable store of material in Chinese, and an excessively uncritical attitude which would accept it too easily and lead to inextricable error. All the traditional material must be used, but used very critically, and used in the Western scientific manner.

The last chapter noted how the main trend of Chinese Marxism led, in the pre-war period already, to a barren and restrictive schematism. It insisted on certain arbitrary stages, and recognised only a restricted range of human motives. Work in the field of the history of land-irrigation in China, and the historical study of its effects, did however lead to wider and more dynamic interpretations. Some Marxists followed this line of inquiry, and accordingly reached a somewhat more open-minded and flexible interpretation. If this went so far as to imply a cyclical interpretation of history, however, or to suggest that different cultures or forms of organisation had intrinsic differences in spiritual or personal value, moral worth, strength of character, etc., or that differences in racial characteristics caused variations which were no less important than the alignment of economic self-interest, they seriously infringed the standards of Marxist orthodoxy. Accordingly they were fought, by adherents of the latter, as an extreme form of treachery.

This was the left wing's loss (or would have been so, had enlightenment in fact been its object), since it was just in those directions—of the description and interpretation of great cyclical movements, the rise and fall of dynasties, cultures, areas and peoples, and of the interplay of higher personal and social motives—that Western and Japanese studies were beginning to make extensive and lively progress on modern lines, whereas the opposing Marxist faction was increasingly settling down to its rigid classifications, imposed by the restrictive and retrogressive position of Marxism in science.

* * *

The above will help to make clear the theoretical equipment available, and the respective value of the various available means of analysis. What light can they shed on Chinese history? It is necessary to begin with the epoch of the Shang or Yin, and Chou Dynasties (*c.* 1500 to 250 B.C.) which is of decisive importance, as being the time when China's life and destiny were first cast in a characteristic mould. In that period were formed all the basic characteristics which were to mature and crystallise in and after the first unification of the country in the Ch'in (220–207 B.C.) and Han (202 B.C.–A.D. 220) and from that time onwards were to govern the whole nature of China's subsequent history.

Wang Kuo-wei was a pioneer in the rationalistic explanation of the differences between Yin and Chou. He showed that the society of the Yin was a clan system based on fraternal inheritance, and that the early Chou society which succeeded it was a family system based on primogeniture and ancestral 'law' or ancestor worship. This, then, was not only a change of dynasty, but a cultural, social and racial change. His basic conception was correct, but Wang Kuo-wei relied too much, for interpreting it further, on sources which he thought were accurately representative of the contemporary position, but which have in recent years been believed to be much later in time, and to have been specially compiled for the purpose of giving a particular interpretation of the earlier period. These are, especially, the Rites of Chou and the Book of Rites.

Kuo Mo-jo was able to give an explanation which stressed the material and economic aspects to a great extent. Subsequent work tended—partly and up to a point—to justify the stress laid on these aspects. Kaizuka established that in the earlier Yin period there was a clan system of classified kinship groups, called 'tribes of many children' (11). Kojima and others show that this society was mainly dependent on agriculture (12). Tung Tso-pin noted that the main titles of rank ('marquis', 'earl', 'viscount', 'baron') of the Chou peerage seem to derive from direct equivalents in the preceding Yin system (13).

From this, however, Kaizuka was able to go much further in showing how these ranks were connected with the system of government and control in the Yin period, which was as follows, according to his evidences. The capital and its neighbourhood (in present-day Honan) formed the direct domains of the royal family and closely associated clans. There, agriculture and stock-raising were conducted with the assistance of some of the Hsia people, the previous inhabitants conquered or replaced by the Shang or Yin (originally invaders from the Shantung area) at some date (about 1500 B.C.). The Shang Dynasty, in its later and more mature phase, changed its name to Yin; the latter name will be used here.

A second zone, 'outside' the metropolitan area mentioned above, was settled by conquered peoples or groups who accepted obligations of paying taxes and rendering military service to the Yin, but seem in other respects to have had something of the standing of 'protected states'. Still farther from the centre, in the outermost 'localities', were independent or unassimilated tribes rendering occasional tribute to the Yin rulers.

The Yin 'marquises' and 'earls' in the outer districts were to supervise the surrounding tribal states or groups. The Chou 'race'—though its origins and earlier history are unsure—emerges as a large tribal entity of this kind, of growing independence, charged with supervising the smaller and inferior groups in the West of the country, and being accorded the title of 'Earl of the West'. It appears that the Chou revolted against the Yin, with the support of the very groups it was supposed to control, taking advantage particularly of the discontent caused among these Western subordinate tribes by the excessive taxation imposed by the Yin.

The conclusion of modern scholarship is that the Chous thereupon established a feudal system for the purpose of controlling, not only the conquered Yin, but also the less civilised Eastern tribes who adhered to them. They took over the 'local' and 'district' system of government from the Yin for this purpose, but made it very much stronger by introducing what might be called a 'vertical' (i.e. patriarchal) gradation of authority instead of the 'horizontal' (i.e. fraternal) pattern of the Yin. However, there must have been a wide overlapping of influences, in both time and space, and the final result may have been a very mixed synthesis of institutions and ideas from a wide variety of groups and tribes.

This mixed system must have evolved gradually, over many centuries of Chou rule; it is unrealistic to suppose that it was introduced on the advent of the Chou Dynasty, ready-made and already finalised. It was the attempt of the Confucians to assume just this—that the older feudal system was instituted in its entirety by the all-wise ancients, by way of divine Revelation—that eventually raised scepticism and reaction against them, in later ages. Scholars of a past generation then concluded that the 'complete and perfect' hierarchical system, from the Five Ranks (the four ranks previously mentioned, plus the 'princes' above them) to the various details of ritual and etiquette, were largely invented by the Confucians for their own purposes, in the Spring and Autumn period (722–481 B.C.).

A more modern view is that the features in question did actually exist in the Yin and Chou epochs; but that they were mixed in their origins and character, and underwent a long and complicated evolution. The Confucians (centuries later) oversimplified them and idealised them, for the purposes of their statecraft—for which they needed, above all, a code of personal and social discipline.

Of special significance, however, is the—very recent—realisation by scholars that the Western portion of the Chou domains, in particular, was the area which was the forcing-ground for all these tendencies, the place and time in which the aboriginal Chinese society, the first in the long chain of development down to the present day, initially took shape. Social and economic history may shed much light on this, the Chinese Genesis, although the historical data are very limited and the conclusions uncertain.

It is concluded that the Chou race established a feudal system to control the Yin race and the Eastern barbaric tribes, in and around what is now Honan. This system very firmly implanted the ideas of dominance and authority, with primogeniture, patriarchalism, respect for age and ancestry. It needed, similarly, to enforce a high degree of centralisation of control and authority, but with a devolution of functions. In the economic sphere, equally, it gave preponderance to the central and metropolitan area, and encouraged centripetal tendencies. The country was arranged in fiefs, like concentric circles around the capital, with the most prosperous and progressive districts nearer the centre, the wilder and less cultivated on the periphery.

All these features were broadly contrary to what had gone before, when the social pattern had been one of clan relations and fraternal connections, the political structure had been rather a federal arrangement of tribal or clan contacts, economic activities had been diffuse and undeveloped; and so forth. As usual in cases of conquest, many groups, individuals, institutions and usages, from among the defeated Yin, were evidently recognised or adopted by the victorious Chou; there were intermarriages also.

But the new pattern and outlook were so strongly and lastingly inculcated that they were to be, ever after, the essential characteristics of the Chinese society and economy: a centralised authoritarianism and metropolitanism, in every aspect of life; economic, social and cultural. They were always contending, however, with centrifugal forces—the growth of wealth, power and dissent in the Localities, the shifts in the internal balance of power.

Further research, in the field of economic history especially, should do much to widen and deepen our understanding of the formative processes involved. We may visualise, as a starting-point, the elders of the Chou aristocracy consolidating their centralised domain, while the sons and younger brothers are posted to the outer districts. There, the latter find a mixed situation. Besides their own people, there are the Yin, there are also other tribes, and there are many varieties of local conditions and peculiarities. As the territory is settled, cleared and developed, local wealth increases and differences with the Centre (the capital and the overlords) intensify, until there is great strife and anarchy, and the economic life is disrupted. It is against this situation that the Confucians protest some centuries later, and they succeed in gaining acceptance for their system and code, which represent a strong reaffirmation of authoritarian centralisation. Then the processes of local development and differentiation begin again, leading to a further period of disintegration; and so on, in an alternating or cyclical movement.

This pattern begins to be traceable from the first dynasties onwards; but, from the beginning, new factors are constantly coming into play. The course of development becomes increasingly complex. The study of the economic aspects, in particular, can do much to extend the understanding of all this. But not if it is used as political Marxism uses it, to exclude all other considerations and impose its own uniformity of conclusions. This tendency is largely accountable for the sterility of historical work on China, in China itself, just at a time when the subject is being greatly broadened and clarified in other lands.

NOTES TO CHAPTER VI

(1) Wittfogel: See Chapter II above, notes 19, 25, 26.

(2) Wittfogel, *Urkommunismus und Feudalismus*, Berlin, 1922; *Geschichte der bürgerlichen Gesellschaft*, Berlin, 1924; 'Entwicklung der Familien-authorität', in *Studien über Autorität und Familie; Schriften des Instituts für Sozialforschung*, v, Paris, 1936; 'Die natürliche Ursachen der Wirtschaftsgeschichte', in *Archiv für Sozialwissenschaft und Sozial-politik*, LXVII, 1932; *Sun Yat Sen*, 1927 (Japanese translation by Tsutsui Eichi, 1932); 'Geopolitik, geographischer Materialismus und Marxismus', in *Unter dem Banner des Marxismus*, III, I–V, 1929 (Japanese translation by Kawanishi Kametaro in *Shiso*, XCVII, 1930); 'Probleme der chinesischen Wirtschaftsgeschichte', in *Archiv für Sozialwissenschaft und Sozialpolitik*, LVII, 1927 (Japanese translation by Yokogawa Jiro, entitled *Shina Keizaishi Kenkyu*, 1935); *Das erwachende China*, Vienna, 1929 (Japanese translation by Nikki Takeshi, 1934).

(3) K. A. Wittfogel and Feng Chia-sheng and others, 'History of Chinese Society (Liao)', *Transactions of the American Philosophical Society*, Philadelphia, XXXVI, 1946. This is a comprehensive work, using practically all the available materials, of all kinds. The value of this work is only slowly beginning to be appreciated in the Far East. First Japanese reactions were that it was too wide, or even indiscriminate. This is partly ascribable to the introductory presentation made by Nohara Shiro, in Bulletin No. 2 of the *Chukoku Kenkyujo*, 1947, which raised mistaken expectations; and partly to the detection of certain alleged errors (e.g. in Khitan inscriptions, which are said to be of recent origin). And it must be noted that the Japanese generally, even their 'synthetists' (among whom outstanding figures are Naito Torajiro, Kato Shigeru, and Mori Shikazo), have insisted on narrower specialisation and stricter interpretation, considering the Columbia-Washington project to be 'over-extended'. Mori Shikazo (see Chapter V, note 8) writes rarely, and is less well known abroad, but has a high scholastic reputation in Japan.

(4) Eberhard, 'Untersuchungen über den Aufbau der chinesischen Kultur. I. Kultur and Siedlung der Randvölker Chinas' (*T'oung Pao*, XXXVI (suppt.) 1942) and 'II. Lokalkulturen im alten China. (1) Kulturen des Nordens und Westens; (2) Kulturen des Nordens und Ostens' (*Monumenta Serica*, III, Peking, 1942).

(5) 'Chinas Geschichte', Bern, 1948; English translation, 'History of China', London, 1950.

(6) Thurnwald, R., *Die menschliche Gesellschaft*, 4 vols., 1935.

(7) See Chapter II, note 24.

(8) O. Lattimore, *Inner Asian Frontiers of China*, 1940; O. and E. Lattimore, *China: a Short History*, 1947.

(9) Liang Ch'i-chao, 1933 (Japanese translation by Hosogaya, 1934). Ch'ien Mu, 1937.

(10) Ikeda Shirojiro, *Keikai Yomoku* (Essentials of Classical Analysis), 1926; *Shoshi Yomoku* (Essentials of the Various Philosophers), 1926.
Yasui Kotaro, *Keigaku Monkei*, 1933.
Nagazawa Noriya, *Shinagaku Nyumonsho Ryakkai*, 1940; *Shinagaku Kankei Nikka-Bun Sanko-sho Ryakusetsu*, 1940; *To-A kankei Sanko-sho Bunken Mokuroku*, 1939.

(11) Kaizuka: See Chapter IV, note 19.

(12) Kojima Sukema, 'Industries of the Yin Period', in *Shinagaku*, III, 10, 1935.
Wu Chi-chang, 'Agricultural Conditions in the Yin period as revealed in inscriptions . . . etc.' (*70th Birthday Essay for Mr. Chang Chu*), 1935.
Hsu Chung-shu, 'On Tillage', *Academia Sinica*, II, 1, 1930.

(13) Tung Tso-pin: See Chapter V, notes 1 and 3.

CHAPTER VII

THE AGE OF CONFUCIUS AND THE CLASSICS

The Chou moved their capital eastward to Loyang, in 770 B.C. Such an event marks the existence of powerful pressure from the West. Thereafter the ruin of the dynasty was very evident; the next period is that of the rise and decline ('Spring and Autumn') of the several Feudal States around the Chou. The ruler of each State began to call himself 'King'. All the old arrangements and values were destroyed or abandoned. The relative positions of the States themselves changed greatly from time to time, but all were armed, and were narrowly intent on an unscrupulous struggle for power and supremacy. The period from 479–255 B.C. is that of the 'Warring States'. One state rose steadily in this period. This was the Ch'in, whose people had moved into the Western area, vacated by the Chou in their eastward migration, and had subsequently built up their strength, by every possible method—military prowess, diplomatic skill, totalitarian discipline, and in other ways—until at last they became the Ch'in Dynasty and unified the country (255–206 B.C.).

Confucius (551–478 B.C.) protested against the conditions of chaos and wickedness that he saw in his own time. He and his followers idealised the more ancient civilisation—in effect, the Yin and Chou systems—and the myths of still more ancient times. Many generations after the death of Confucius, in the reign of Wu Ti of Han (140–87 B.C.), his followers succeeded in establishing their doctrines as the code of official polity, the State religion, and the general morality.

The above is the conventional thumb-nail sketch of a history of some eight centuries, during which period the 'permanent' or underlying characteristics, not only of Chinese civilisation or culture in the abstract, but also of the country's actual livelihood and practical institutions, were fully evolved. All of this can only be explained and understood by a very great extension of studies in the social history of China in general, and of its economic aspects in particular. Such a study can only be fruitful, however, if it is undertaken in the spirit of a very full realisation of the complexity of the subject, the infinite variety of forms and motives at work, and the uncertainty of almost all the evidence. It can only be successful if it displays a due humility, in face of the vast mass of data presented—in any one single period alone—and recognises that all efforts and conclusions must remain tentative, for a long time to come.

The qualities of the now dominant Marxism are the exact reverse of all those just mentioned. It is sweeping, arrogant, assertive, dogmatic; its pattern is ready-made, and it is concerned merely to fit any new evidence into its existing categories. If these fail, its pseudo-philosophical apparatus is always ready to hand, with the aid of which any difficulties can be dismissed, by the kind of 'dialectical' double-talk in which everything is its own antithesis, and progress is defined as the negation of a negation. It is a very great tragedy for China that such a thraldom should have fallen upon her just as the defects and limitations of the older dogmatism were being left behind.

A full picture could only come from a great number of regional studies. Such completeness may now be unattainable, because the local and special records may not be sufficiently preserved. But the analysis of the main issues and general aspects may still be energetically and profitably pursued in those lands where thought and scholarship remain free and active.

In the period referred to above, many distinct and important phases may be distinguished. The decline of Chou, as a centralised or centripetal polity and economy. The rise (economic, social or cultural) of the peripheral states; their interrelation, and their subsequent decline. The rise of Ch'in; its new features, and the nature of the new dictatorship which it finally introduced. Each of these phases has a myriad facets, and all the parts of the story interlock; our present knowledge gives merely a skeleton and an outline of all that is involved.

Consider the numerous types of approach that are open to the analyst. They have been amply used already, as shown by the bibliographies below. One is a 'geopolitical' treatment, in terms of geography and strategy. Concerning such shifts as the eastward movement of Chou, there are many writings from this point of view (1). There is a point of view which is more strictly 'political', concerning itself (in regard to the same period) with the nature of the Chou feudalism (2). A third approach may be called 'anthropological', taking religion and custom, and all that they imply (3). This leads on directly to the 'ecological' considerations of how these people lived and adapted themselves to their environment (4).

None of these can proceed far without entering into considerations of economic history, 'pure' or 'proper'. The main specific topics under this heading (for the period now in question) should now be mentioned. A central problem is that of the 'well-field' system, which must be considered in conjunction with the complementary features of the taxation system contextually mentioned by Mencius: 'tribute', 'aid' and 'service' (5). If these were fully understood, we should know what were the relations between the Chou aristocracy and its farmer-subordinates, and how those relations developed; and we should know also what broadly was the technique of agriculture (6). The account given by Mencius is surely legendary, but it must dimly reflect some image of the past, as well as exemplifying some proposals for reform in Mencius' own day.

The Spring and Autumn period, and that of the Warring States, saw local concentrations of power replacing the former centralisation. But clearly, there were accompanying changes of structure internally, within the respective states. In the process of state-building (generally conducted on principles entirely Machiavellian), local districts were more intensively cultivated, local production was stimulated; advantages began to appear in local specialisation, each area promoting the products to which it was better suited. A corollary was increasing trade, increasing use of money, accumulation of capital, and its reinvestment. But the medium of permanent reinvestment, to which the accumulated cash came in the end, was land. So far the general similarity with European history is close. But the concept and the practice of sovereignty differed from that of early Europe. The evolution in China at this phase clearly omitted the 'manorial' stage, at least as a political or state-forming factor. The agrarian relationships were in the nature of those existing on large estates (7).

The Marxist representation of 'serfdom' or 'slavery'—concepts drawn from European antecedents and connotations—as characteristics of this early Chinese society, are accordingly of special absurdity. Hardly less inapposite is the rest of its preconceived—and similarly European-based—class structure, postulating lords and bondsmen. There certainly exist ancient Chinese words translatable as 'slave', 'serf', 'subject', etc., but these terms evidently bore a different connotation from the European ones.

Modern research attributes increasingly significant roles, in the dynamics of the Chinese society of that epoch, to certain classes or types of retainers, declassed persons, and intermediaries of various kinds. These show important and interesting differences from any analogies in other national histories (though analogies do exist, e.g. troubadours in Europe, ronin in Japan). They seem chiefly to have been itinerants and adventurers. Such were the 'House Guests' who attached themselves to aristocratic households. Those representing the intelligentsia are termed 'dialecticians' or magicians; those who were men-at-arms are known as 'cavaliers' (8). Some modern scholars are able to relate these elements fairly directly to the evolution of social and political thought in the period (9).

The 'personalisation' of early Chinese history resulting from such work is at least a refreshing counterbalance to the more largely mechanistic views presented by the Wittfogel-Chi Ch'ao-ting school, which traces the process of state-building as conditioned by the large-scale discipline and organisation involved in major operations of flood-control and irrigation, and of those who trace the evolution of local and regional government, as the framework of development (10).

* * *

It is perhaps time to restate a warning given at the outset: that the present treatise does not purport to give an account or narrative of the Economic History of China, but only to assess the importance of the subject, the position it has reached, its problems and perspectives of development. Incidentally, it presents a very wide bibliography of the subject.

The bibliography is vast. It is time that a co-ordinated effort was made, on an international scale, to collate, digest and simplify the whole mass of material. The student is faced with entries like '*General Catalogue of the Four Divisions of the Imperial Library*, in 200 volumes; even the 'concise' summary of this, in a mere twenty volumes, may seem a monumental book list (11). In the case of basic references and catalogues like the above, it is, however, generally sufficient to be aware of their existence, so that they may be used in case of need or opportunity. Besides the extensive lists of books and monographs, there are many lists of articles and other minor references in Chinese, Japanese and European languages; a selection from each category is given below (12).

For the actual reading list, the student should at an early stage give priority to the best works of general introduction, which explain the nature of Sinological literature, and the way in which it is to be handled. Suggestions in this respect are also given below (13).

NOTES TO CHAPTER VII

(1) Fu Ssu-nien, 'Major and Minor Eastward Movements, *A.S.*, II, 1, 1932; 'Chou Odes . . .', *A.S.*, I, 1, 1930.
Ch'i Ssu-ho, 'The theory that Yen and Wu were not feudatories of Chou', in *Yenching Bulletin*, XXVIII, 1940.
Hu Hou-hsuan, 'Easterly origin of the Chou', *Peking University Historical Review*, I, 1934.
Kaizuka: See Chapter IV, note 19.

(2) Okazaki Fumio, *Kodai Shina Shi Yomoku*, 1943.
Miura Shinshichi, 'Group Consciousness in Ancient China', in *Tosei Bunmeishi Ronko* (Study of History of Eastern and Western Civilisations), 1950.
Kato Shigeru, 'On the Feudal System of China', in *Shakai Keizai Shigaku*, VII, 9, 1937.
Hashimoto Masukichi, 'Feudal System of Ancient China', in *Chukoku Kodai Bunka-shi Kenkyu*, 1948.

(3) Kato Tsuneyoshi: See Chapter VI.
Kojima Sukema, *Shina Kodai Kenkyu*, 1943.

Yamada Wataru, 'The T'ien Sha concept and the State Policy', in *Kyodo Kenkyu Kodai Kokka*, 1949; 'Patriarchal names and Matrimonial relationships in Tso's Commentary', in *Kangaku-kai Zasshi*, v to ix, 1948–9.

Shigezawa Toshiro, 'Belief in gods in the Spring and Autumn period', in *Shinagaku*, ix, 2, 1941.

Fujieda Ryoei, 'Primitive Ecology of the Deities', in *Shinagaku*, x, 2, 1942.

Matsumoto Nobuhiro, *Kodai Bunka Ron*, 1932.

E. Chavannes, *Le dieu du sol dans la Chine antique*, Paris, 1910.

M. Granet, *Fêtes et chansons de la Chine ancienne*, Paris, 1919 (Japanese translation by Uchida Tomo-o, 1932); *Civilisation chinoise*, 1926 (English translation by Innes and Brailsford, 1930); *Danses et Légendes de la Chine ancienne*, 1926; *La Religion chinoise*, 1922 (Japanese translation by Tsumura Itsuo, 1942); *La polygynie sororale et le sororat dans la China féodale*, 1920.

Ting Wen-chiang, review of Granet's 'Chinese Civilisation', *C.S.P.S.R.*, xv, 3, 1931.

(4) Karlgren, 'Legends and Cults in Ancient China', *Bulletin of Museum of Far Eastern Antiquities*, xviii, Stockholm, 1946.

(5) Kato Shigeru, *Shina Kodensei no Kenkyu* (Field-System of Ancient China), 1916.

Ogawa Takuji, 'Free fields and farms, and the Well-field', in *Shina Rekishi Chiri Kenkyu Zokushu*, 1929.

Hashimoto Masukichi, 'Study of the Field-system in Ancient China', in *Chukoku Kodai Bunka Kenkyu*, 1947. Miyazaki Ichisada, 'Tax-system of Ancient China', in *Shirin*, xviii, 2–4, 1933.

Wu Chi-chang, 'History of the Chinese Field-system in the pre-Ch'in period', in *Wuhan University Sociological Quarterly*, v, July–August 1935.

Kao Yun-hui, 'Land-system and Well-field in the Chou period', in *Shih Huo*, i, 6, 1935.

(6) Hsu Chung-shu, *On Tillage* (see Chapter VI, note 12).

Nishida Tamotsu, 'Agriculture of Ancient China', in *Rekishi Kyoiku*, viii, 3, 1933.

(7) Kojima Sukema, 'Origin of Trade', in *Kodai Shina Kenkyu*, Kyoto, 1943; 'Money economy in the Spring and Autumn period', in *Shinagaku*, vi, 7, 1938.

Miyazaki Ichisada, 'On the Origin of Trade', in *Toyoshi Kenkyu*, v, 4, 1939.

Ho Han, 'Evolution of Merchants during the Warring States period', in *Shih Huo*, ii, 5, 1935.

(8) Tao Hsi-sheng, *Dialecticians and Cavaliers*, 1931.

(9) Kojima Sukema, 'Social and Economic Thought of Ancient China', in *Kodai Shina Kenkyu*, 1943.

Kimura Eiichi: see notes to Chapter IV.

Hodzumi Fumio, *Sen-So Keizai Shiso Shi* (History of pre-Ch'in Economic Thought), 1942.
T'ang Ching-tseng, 1936.

(10) Ku Chieh-kang, 'Hsien (counties) in the Spring and Autumn period', in *Tribute of Yu*, VII, 6–7, 1937.
D. Bodde, *China's First Unifier*, Leyden, 1938. (Appendix: 'Rise of the Hsien and Chun Systems'.)
Chung Feng-nien, 'Territorial Changes during the Warring States period', in *Tribute of Yu*, VI, 10, 1936, and VII, 6–7, 1937.

(11) *General Catalogue*, 200 vols. (foreign-style binding, moveable-type edition, Commercial Press); *Summary*, 20 vols.

(12) Japanese, *Catalogue of Chinese books in the Toho Bunka Kenkyujo*, 1945, and the same Institute's (Otsuka Historical Association) *Toyoshi Ronbun Yomoku* (List of Articles on Oriental History), 1936 (6 vols.). In 1932, the Harvard-Yenching Press produced an *Index to articles on Oriental studies in 38 kinds of Japanese periodicals* (in China), followed by a supplement (covering 175 Japanese periodicals in China) in 1940. The (Kyoto) Jimbun Kagaku Kenkyujo is currently producing its excellent bibliographies. Another very famous source is the (Kobe) Yamaguchi Kosho *Toyo Kankei Tosho Mokuroku*.
In Chinese: Peking Library, 1934–6 (Wang Yung and Mao Naiwens editors), 'Articles on Chinese Geography'; and *ibid.*, 1929–36, 'Article, on Chinese Studies'.
Western: a classic is H. Cordier's *Bibliotheca Sinica*, 5 vols., 1909–24, reprinted Pelping, 1938.
C. S. Gardner, *Union List of selected books on China in American Libraries*, 1938.

(13) See also Chapter V, note 8, and Chapter VI, note 9.
Liang Ch'i-chao: See Chapter VI, note 9.
C. S. Gardner, *Chinese Traditional Historiography*, 1938.
Ishida Mikinosuke, author of the excellent historical novel, *Choan no Haru* (*Spring in Chang An*), 1941; *Ojin no Shina-Kenkyu* (*European studies of China*), 1932, revised ed. 1946; and *Obei ni okeru Shina-kenkyu*, 1942.
Social and Economic History Society of Japan (Shakai Keizai Shigaku Kai), *Shakai Keizai Shigaku no Hattatsu*, 1941.
Ando Hideo, '20 years of Oriental Studies in the Soviet Union', in *Moko*, January 1941.

CHAPTER VIII

THE FIRST UNIFICATION OF CHINA: ITS POLITICAL AND SOCIAL BACKGROUND

The Ch'in (255–209 B.C.) and Han (206 B.C.–A.D. 220) were the first periods of political unification in China. From the political point of view, they may be taken to represent the starting-point in the story of China, the Nation—an entity, an individuality. They set the pattern of self-centredness, in respect especially of foreign relations; they gave an introvert character to the national psychology, which may or may not be peculiar to China among all the nations, but certainly took a special and lasting form there.

It is still far from clear whether that self-centredness, or collective egotism—expressed in the very name of the country, as the 'Middle Kingdom' (Chung Kuo)—is a basic feature in the national character, or just a form of words, a conventional expression. Politically, at least, some such outlook was strongly imparted in the periods now in question, and strongly retained ever since.

The appearances are that few if any countries had, historically, their first unification in so sudden and thorough a form as did China under the Ch'in. This (and the reign of Wang Mang, A.D. 9–23) were indeed totalitarianism, of a kind or degree fully comparable to those occurring in Europe some nineteen centuries later. However, the long period of the Former and Later Han, which followed, must have done far more to fix the lasting outlook of the Empire. The Han, besides consolidating the internal unity of China, developed the country's external relations, to the point of asserting the predominance of China as a relatively isolated, brilliantly cultured nation-state, surrounded by comparatively barbarous peoples on a merely tribal level with whom its contacts were partial and irregular. The same characteristics (of brilliance, suzerainty and centrality) were equally pronounced in the T'ang period (seventh to tenth centuries). The Sung, the Ming and the Manchus, with diminishing success, strove later to revive these attributes.

In the periods between, however, there were intervals of disruption, defeat, invasion, subjection and decay. The key to the understanding of Chinese history is now generally held to be a comprehension of the respective groups of forces (external and exogenous, such as foreign conquest and pressures on the frontiers, and internal or endogenous, the processes of decline and collapse within); and also of the interaction or interplay between all these.

From the point of view of political and cultural history, all this ground has been rather fully worked over. From the point of view of social history, the ground has been less fully covered; but present-day scholarship is bent on remedying that defect. Analysis of the sociological aspects and implications of all this will do much to transform what has for the most part (because of the largely 'political' treatment) been seen in silhouette, into a three-dimensional drama of human figures 'in the round'. Only by taking a social historian's view can we determine the phases and the motive forces in each period, saying (for instance) which aspects of a particular dynastic order were inherent and well-founded, and which were artificial and declining; or showing which aspects of an invading or conquering group were merely negative, destructive of another, and which were positive, in the sense of contributing a fresh element or leading to a new synthesis.

Political history can be misleading, if it focuses too much attention on the innovations, on the entirely new features, and on the actual moment of change. Usually these are only the outward and visible signs of inner and deeper processes. The viewpoint of social history furnishes a valuable corrective, in showing the underlying continuity, and the essentially evolutionary nature of the processes involved. Thus, the preceding chapters may have shown, in respect of the first dynasties of China, a developing pattern of accretion. More and more diverse elements were added, included and absorbed as time went on; at that early stage, already, Chinese civilisation was complex and many-sided. This process was to be continued, and enormously extended, in subsequent epochs. The Han period is the first of a number of such tremendous extensions thereafter. A view of history which seeks always to reduce it to the lowest common denominator is therefore a false one, antithetical to the interests of enlightenment and the requirements of accuracy.

Such a view is that which rules that 'all history is the history of class struggle'. The supporters of this interpretation are intent on reducing each period to a direct clash of two main factors or parties. Idealising the act of revolution, they focus an excessive and misleading attention on the instant of change, and on the factors which favour the change. They depreciate (and vilify) the factors directly opposing the change. All other factors, other than the selected 'thesis' and the predetermined 'antithesis', they strive to ignore, or to discount to the point of unimportance.

This is the great danger facing economic history today, especially in the case of China. The subject of economic history is seized upon by Marxism, which makes 'economic forces' the main or determinant consideration of history, and subjects the whole study to the narrowing process above described. This is an obscurantist use of what should be a principal means of enlightenment. For economic history, in its proper and wide use, offers a real means of clarification in the field of Chinese history. It can show, in terms of basic livelihood and the closest realities of progress, the actual nature of the social relations. The economic factor is not the one which determines all others, it is rather the point at which all other human considerations meet; only in this sense is it a common denominator.

The usefulness of economic history is conditional on the user's recognition of the width and variety of its implications, of the number and complexity of the social forces involved, and of the fact that economic features are not always the causal ones, but may just as well be effects, the causes of which must be sought in other fields. If these things are not recognised, the result is that economic history becomes a means of obscuring and distorting history, for some political purpose.

This is clearly evident, in respect of the period of Chinese history now under consideration. The limit of historical absurdity seems to be reached when the theory and the terminology specially devised to explain European history, and to do so from the particular point of view of exhorting

European factory-workers to revolt in the nineteenth century, is applied indiscriminately to such remote conditions. This is probably not, however, the most dangerous aspect of the Marxian doctrine, in the field of history. Its first rule of practice is the persistent and uncompromising vilification of all past periods, to support the contention that the regime now ruling is the first to represent true 'progress', or the interest of 'the people'. Its second rule of practice is that any progress or enlightenment, in any previous period, may only be attributed to persons or groups who can in some way be made to appear equivalent to the present-day party or its contemporary leaders, or can be hailed as forerunners of the same.

* * *

The age of Confucius and the classics, briefly referred to in the last chapter, was an age of sharp struggles and polemics. So much so, perhaps, that it must inevitably be treated in a polemical or partisan manner. In approaching the succeeding age, however, the purpose and the treatment must be explanatory; the Han age, at any rate, represented a new and broadly based equilibrium, with great and lasting consequences. Moreover, the data became, henceforward, more definitely historical.

The first and most fundamental references for the student should therefore be such minor classics as the *Historical Records* of Ssu-ma Ch'ien, the *Han History* of Pan Ku, and the *History of the Later Han* of Fan Yeh (1), and the extensive annotations on these by the critics of the Ch'ing Dynasty, which are mainly philological in their scope and intention (2). Moreover, there are excellent European translations of the basic texts themselves (3). In Japanese, there is an excellent translation of the sections which are of major interest from the point of view of economic history (or social and economic history) by Kato Shigeru, including the *Money and Industry*, *Biographies*, and *Literature of Market Stabilisation* sections of the *Historical Records*, and the *Food and Money* part of the Han History (4). And the Japanese writers Okazaki and Naito have very skilfully and adequately presented the setting and the perspective of this group of classical writings (5). The extensive criticism, in China and

Japan, shows that the *Historical Records* is the most questionable of these sources (6).

Besides the orthodox histories, there are numerous works of chronology (7), and attempts to classify or codify the legal and institutional features of the times (8). There is also a profusion of relics and inscriptions from this period: inscriptions on metal and stone (9) and wooden tablets (10). The wooden tablets found at Chuyen in Sinkiang in 1929–30, by Bergman and his Chinese colleagues, are much more comprehensive as records than the earlier finds of Aurel Stein, and shed much light on the contemporary social organisation. Lau Kan has shown how they may be effectively used in that direction (11). Besides the metal and stone inscriptions, there are two other important types of direct evidence on this period: inscribed clay tablets, and official seals, the study of which gives much information on the geography, administration and other aspects of the period (12).

When we come to the Han period, furthermore, we find a considerable amount of original and contemporary writings and discussions on economic and social problems of the time; the close study of these is an urgent necessity for economic historians in the West (13). Oriental scholars have produced some useful materials on this (14).

The basic problem, in the study of the Ch'in and Han era, is to know how the strong political centralisation was related to the social and economic structure of society. In the rise of Ch'in, from its initial position as a tribal state in the west, to victory over the Six States and the establishment of the unified First Empire, various factors must be involved. Its centralised system of government, establishing a scheme of districts and counties quite different from the loose feudal structure of Chou, has attracted the particular attention of the scholars. Formally, it was a triumph of legalist thought, the policy of deliberate nation-building being based on the teachings of Han Fei Tzu and his school and put into practice by Li Ssu (15). But the inspiration for these thoughts and deeds must also be traced to some earlier antecedents; the analogy and example of the rise of Chou, and the leadership of Lord Shang, are especially considered by Oriental writers (16).

The basic economic measures enforced by Li Ssu seem evidently rational and productive; standardisation of wheel-gauges, of weights and measures, of ways of writing, of currency (by the introduction of the half-tael). Li Ssu's purely political measures, and some that might belong to either field —e.g. the compulsory migration of powerful local clans to the centre—seem realistic and well calculated. Why did his system break down, with local groups clearly formed, and ready to revolt as soon as a Liu Pang arose to bring the First Empire to its end?

Modern research is showing that a great variety of social forces were at work. The attempt to pin the labels 'revolutionary' on any particular social groups or classes of the period, is becoming increasingly futile; no less so, the attempt to equate these supposed classes with any distinct or consistent basis of economic position or economic interests. Some small but powerful clans functioned stably as upholders of local order; others were in constant movement and opposition to the regime. The conditions of land-ownership do not seem to have affected this relationship. Racial and clan feelings mainly affected the alignment. An extraordinary influence was wielded by the vagabond intelligentsia, who were surprisingly numerous and successful in this period. Some of them continued in the traditions of the dialecticians, magicians and cavaliers mentioned in the previous period, but the name for the genus, in the Ch'in-Han period now under consideration, is 'House Guests'. And they appear to have changed in function, as well as in name, now figuring as leaders or instigators of movements and intrigues in nation-wide politics. They cannot be associated with any particular economic function, or economic interest. They served all manner of masters, and their nature and behaviour varied accordingly. Under landlords or rich men of plebeian and non-aristocratic origin, we find them promoting various local and clan interests. Under the aristocrats of the Six States, we find them typically concerned with promoting the powers and functions of the states (usually inconsistent with the clan and district interests). Under the city 'heroes' (township leaders) we find them operating as secret policemen, terrorists, propagandists, bureaucrats and other instruments of a local rule so direct that usually it meant a local dictatorship. Finally, they were associated also with thieves and robbers, participating directly in the bands of marauders (17).

It is a tenable thesis that material conditions were so bad, in the chaotic period of the Warring States, that generally they could not get worse. It is a tenable thesis, though somewhat contradictory to the last-mentioned one, that the era was one of considerable local development; and that the newly developed and enriched local interests were, in some senses, in conflict with some of the central interests in and around the Court. It seems to be distinctly true that the solution advanced by the Confucians was a return to the older models, the original feudalism of Chou. This solution did not necessarily involve suppression of the 'rising merchant class'; though such suppression, by sumptuary laws, constant and elaborate legislation limiting personal expenditure, etc., had been a main feature of the whole preceding period.

The indications are that the Ch'in (and again Wang Mang) achieved a political, formal and superficial unification, but that the forces and relations involved were extremely complex. The Han Dynasty achieved a new and lasting, but no less elaborate, equilibrium. It seems futile to try to detect in all this, any consistent or coherent alignments on a 'class' basis. Fluidity and variety, constant experiment and adoption of new ideas and ways, have been the signs of progress, in the history of China as much as that of any other country. Equally, the periods when thought and usage have been regimented and dictated have been those of greatest decline and distress. This is as true today as it was nearly two thousand years ago.

NOTES TO CHAPTER VIII

(2) Takigawa Kametaro's, in *Toyo Bunka Gakuho*, 1942.
(3) H. H. Dubs, *History of the Former Han by Pan Ku*, 2 vols., 1938, 1944. E. Chavannes, *Mémoires historiques de Se-Ma Ts'ien*, 5 vols., Paris, 1895–1905.
(4) Kato Shigeru, *Annotated Translations*, Iwanami Bunko, 1942.

(5) Okazaki Fumio, *Shina Shigaku Shiso no Hattatsu*, Iwanami Bunko, 1935. Naito Konan (Torajiro), *Chukoku Shigaku Shi*, 1949.

(6) Li Kuei-yao, *Tsing Hua Journal*, IV, 1.
Okazaki Fumio, *Ssu-Ma Ch'ien*, 1947. Takeda Yasuatsu, *Ssu-Ma Ch'ien*, 1943.

(7) Hsuen Yueh; Yuan Hung (Of Chin); Wang I-chih of Sung.

(8) Hsu T'ien-lin of Sung; Wang Yin-ling of Sung; Sun Hsing-yen of Ch'ing; Ch'eng Shu-teh, 1927.
Takigawa Masajiro, 'Modern Studies of Han Law', in *Shigaku Zasshi*, LII, 4, 1942.

(9) Wang Chang of Ch'ing; Yung Ken, 'Metal Inscriptions of Han, Ch'in, and Miscellaneous Items', *A.S.*, V, 1931.

(10) E. Chavannes, *Documents . . . découverts par Aurel Stein . . .*, 1913. Lo Chen-Yu and Wang Kuo-wei, 1914; and a further supplement by Wang Kuo-wei in 1916.

(11) Lau Kan, 'Preface to the study of the Han tablets . . .', in *A.S.*, X, 1935; *Study of the Han Tablets. . . .* 6 vols., 1944; 'Military System of the Han', in *A.S.*, X, 1935; 'Economic Life West of the Yellow River, as recorded in the Han tablets', *A.S.*, XI, 1936.

(12) Lo Chen-yu, 1913. Wang Kuo-wei, 'Investigation of Tablets', in *Literary Relics of Prince Hatming and Duke Chung-I*, II. Hsu Chien of Ch'ing (ed.), 2 vols.
Chai Chung-yun of Ch'ing, 17 vols.

(13) Chia Yi, *New Writings*. Huan K'uan, *Discourses on Salt and Iron*. Wang Chung.
Yen Ko-chun of Ch'ing (ed.), *Complete Collection. . . .*
'Wang Han'.
Annotations on the *Discourses on Salt and Iron*, by Lu Wen-shao, Chang Tun-jen, Wang Hsien-ch'ien and (best) Hsu Teh-pei. Japanese translation by Sogabe Shizuo (Iwanami, 1934). English translation by E. M. Gale, 1931.

(14) Ma Fei-po, articles in *Shih Huo*, 1934–5, 'Data for the Economic History of Ch'in and Han' (*Manufacture*, II, 8; *Commerce*, II, 10; *Agriculture*, III, 1; *Money*, III, 2; *Population and Land*, III, 3; *Slavery*, III, 8; *Taxation*, III, 9).
T'ao Hsi-sheng, *Economic History of the Western Han*, 1931.
Ma Cheng-feng, *Economic History of China*, II, 1936.
Chien Pai-tsan, 'History of Ch'in and Han', in *Studies of Chinese History*, II, 1947.

(15) D. Bodde, *China's First Unifier*, Leyden, 1938.
Shih Hai-nien, 'The Ch'in County System', in *Tribute of Yu*, VII, 6–7, Ch'ien Mu, 'The 36 Districts of Ch'in', in *Tsing Hua Weekly*, XXXVII, 9–10; and further study of this subject in *Tribute of Yu*, VII, 6–7.

(16) Kimura Eiichi, 'Studies on Legalist Thought', 1944.
Liu Tao-yun, 'Shang Yang's reform . . .', in *Shih Huo*, I, 3, 1934.
Kimura Masao, 'Free Fields and Farms', in *Shicho*, XII, 2, 1937.

(17) T'ao Hsi-sheng, 'House Guests of the Western Han', in *Shih Huo*, v, 1, 1938; 'Powerful Clans . . . in the later years of Wang Mang', *ibid.*, v, 6; *Dialecticians and Cavaliers*, 1931.

Chu Ching-yuan, 'House Guests in the Three Kingdoms', in *Shih Huo*, v, 6; 'House Guests, Disciples, etc. . . .', *ibid.*, II, 1934.

Nishijima Sadao, 'Observations on the Formation of the Chinese Empire', in *Rekishigaku Kenkyu*, 141.

Utsunomiya Kiyoyoshi, 'Households and Clans in the Han Dynasty', in *Shirin*, XXIV, 2.

Yang Lien-sheng, 'Powerful Clans of the Eastern Han', in *Tsing Hua Journal*, x, 4.

CHAPTER IX

THE GREAT HAN EMPIRE

As noted in the preceding chapter, the concrete and historical evidence about China becomes much clearer and more plentiful, as we go from the earliest times to the Han Dynasty; thereafter the treatment may be increasingly historical, and not merely inferential (though the inferential analysis still remains important). Some evidence has been offered in the foregoing of the great degree to which the original Chinese civilisation developed by a process of accretion, in a highly eclectic manner. In an extremely fluid and changeful process, all sorts of components and methods were adopted, mingled, varied and fused from a great mixture of races, political, social and philosophical or religious ideas, systems of administration, production, etc., all in a constant state of flux.

Externally, the very size and shape of the country, the society and the economy, changed repeatedly and constantly, with varying 'frontiers' (political, social, economic and cultural) against the surrounding 'barbarian' elements, unassimilated or partly-assimilated, under each heading. Internally, the structure of the unit (under each of the same headings) was equally variable, similarly representing at each time a different equilibrium between a variety of forces or components. 'The Middle Kingdom' was in those ages a relative, not an absolute, conception of centrality. A wide view was taken of the world as 'Everything under Heaven', comprising a wondrous diversity of persons and trends; the 'middle' state was at any time the area which was temporarily in balance between the more extreme forces. The conception was not fixed in terms of any geographical limits, or of any sacrosanct way of life, or outlook; it did not assume any permanent self-containedness, social, cultural or economic.

In the progressive unification of the country under the Chou, Ch'in and Han, political and cultural 'metropolitanism' was increasingly the form, with increasing stress on political and economic centralisation. From the Han time onwards a more set and accepted pattern, and traditional or conventional norms, appeared permanently to prevail; they defined a more unvarying pattern, in which China seems more or less 'statically' to have continued until comparatively recent times.

This would seem to be only partly or relatively true; in most of the succeeding centuries, there were manifold innovations and adjustments, and (though the successive equilibria became broader-based and more lasting) the position continued usually to be one of a changing balance. The picture of inertia or stagnation, the kind of dull longevity against which the English poet protested with his 'better fifty years of Europe than a cycle of Cathay', is only partly true; or it relates to some special period such as the heyday of the Manchu Dynasty (say the later eighteenth and early nineteenth centuries).

If a warning is required against this negative view expressed by some 'bourgeois' observers, it must be said that the now widespread Marxist approach tends somewhat in the same direction. How laughable, in face of the extent, variety and complexity of Chinese history, is the view that 'all history is the history of class struggle', in the sense that all history is interpretable (alike, and with finality, by a Marx in 1848, a Lenin in 1918, a Stalin in 1938 and a Mao in 1948) in terms of a common and basically unchanged pattern of class conflicts, in which the economic factor is always and everywhere the decisive one. As will be seen below, this leads essentially to the Marxist analyst having to classify a vast period of Chinese history, from as early as the lifetime of Confucius to as late as that of Generalissimo Chiang Kai-shek, as the 'feudal' or 'medieval' period. At best, this occasions an inert and negative treatment; in some cases the effect is rather like that of a guide-book to an ancient city which would describe the ground on which it is built, and the flag on its roof-top, briefly remarking of the rest that it was a feudal and medieval structure for the oppression of the people, but is now the site for a new People's City.

* * *

There was a great transition, a deep change in the nature of the country, from the era of Contending States (fifth and fourth centuries B.C.) to the consolidation of the Han Dynasty (from about two centuries later). It may be appropriate to point the contrast in terms of the personality and career of the chief leaders in the process of nation-building. Li Ssu, the Unifier of the Ch'in period (256–207 B.C.), worked in and through the personal ruler of the Ch'in state, advising and serving his Prince directly; analogies might be drawn with Machiavelli, Richelieu or others in European history. Hsiang Yu, who rose in revolt against Ch'in, was a refugee aristocrat from Ch'u; he relied to a considerable extent on the services of 'vagrant cavaliers' on a lower social plane, and on enlisting the support of local clans. Liu Pang, who was more successful in the same effort, overthrowing the Ch'in and becoming the first Han Emperor, was of lower social origin, the son of a local official. He and his successors used the same techniques (cultivating advisers and premiers who contributed statecraft, and adventurers who gave physical and practical support) but leant more heavily on support from the commoners, the traders and other lower classes of the time.

The early Han rulers had to adopt Centralism, in imitation of their predecessors, as their legal framework and their basis of government. But it may be said that, having strongly in mind the failure of Ch'in, they established first a mixed system combining various antecedents—the 'district' system ('counties' and 'commanderies') which was also 'feudal' (rewarding faithful lieutenants with fiefs)—moving later to a fuller political unification, appointing competent legal and administrative officers of all kinds, but to a notable extent from the lower classes. The policy of the early Han was pragmatic rather than principled.

A struggle between the 'new gentry' and the 'new feudal lords' ensued. The class of gentry were successful; and a system of their practical rule under dynastic patronage was imposed, which has certainly coloured Chinese history ever since. With the adoption of Confucianism, from the third century B.C., their dominance was fixed in the pattern of learned traditionalism, and they may be described as the 'scholar-gentry' (1).

Work in the field of economic history can do a great deal

to clarify the background and the basis of these developments; first of all in identifying the internal situation in China at that time, the main factors and motives at work, and second (probably to a lesser extent) in analysing the external relations of Han China, which became increasingly important with the spread of that luxuriant Empire to the west and south. Fortunately some very good work is now going forward in that field. An excellent and fundamental contribution from America is the full translation and annotation of the economic portions of the Han history by Miss Swann of Princeton. Vivid and useful as an introductory work, on the corresponding material, is a recent article by Miss Blue in the Harvard Journal (2).

Concerning the Twenty-four Dynastic Histories generally, it must be borne in mind that each is essentially a piece of official political propaganda, concerned to justify the dynasty under which it was written.

From this point of view, it is particularly important to analyse the evidences concerning the institution, in the early Han period, of the village administrative and economic system, including such key features as the 'Three Elders', 'Youthful Talents', 'Field Works', etc. (3). Studies could next be developed on the taxation and public finance system of the Han. In the subsequent period, this was perhaps the aspect in which the unification policy bore with increasing severity on the people's livelihood, destroying whatever popularity or stability may have been gained by the earlier social and administrative measures on the village level, referred to in the last sentence (4). An associated heading is that of compulsory labour and military service, exactions under which worked to the same effect to undermine the social basis of Han China (5).

The third heading for the attention of the economic historians, in respect of this period, might be the nature and composition of the powerful clans, with reference especially to the problems of landownership (6). The development of trade and markets, which had been phenomenally great since the end of the Warring States period, seems to have been a main factor in strengthening and enriching the powerful clans and local interests. The latter seem increasingly to have acquired land, expanded their holdings and displaced farmers (or is it truer to say 'absorbed' them?). On the other hand, the greatly increasing needs of the central government budget, the various needs of public finance, seem to have pressed from above on the locally powerful classes—who evidently passed on this pressure, in turn, to the classes under them.

As in European history, the rise of the nation-state is directly associated with the increase in the state budget and the consequent conflicts of interest. The budgetary needs of the monarchy or the state increase as a rule with the general increase of wealth and display, the natural increase in the scale and needs of administration, and with the increasing scale and cost of wars, foreign relations and expeditions, defensive or aggressive. In Han China, the budget increased for all these reasons; so more and more taxation and labour service were required. It seems that the monarchy and its metropolitan government used these measures in conjunction with a policy of checking or suppressing the growth of local powers.

The last-mentioned struggle would appear also to have mainly an economic aspect. Prominent, or best-known, in this respect are the reigns of the Emperor Wu (141–86 B.C.), and of Wang Mang and Kuang Wu (A.D. 9–57), from which we have an extensive literature of original and derived material; for example that dealing with the famous debate on the state monopoly in salt and iron, and many other aspects of the government's control and anti-mercantile policies (7). The last-named group of material is the best-known to Western students, but in the East useful studies have been pursued to a comparable extent on contingent aspects, other than commerce and government controls, which may be no less important for an understanding of the period: namely, the contemporary agrarian problems (8), development of commerce and industries (9), development of the money economy (10), the family system and the particular problem of domestic slavery (11).

In speaking of local and provincial groupings, the term 'clan' has advisedly been used above, to stress for Western readers that the bonds uniting these groups—by intermarriage, kinship, inheritance, friendship, etc.—were closer and more personal, but also more institutional, than is readily understood from some of the terms more commonly applied, such as 'clique' or 'faction'.

Wang Mang, whose reign from A.D. 9–23 as 'the Socialist Emperor' forms a celebrated break and interlude in the long history of the Han, came to power by the same methods of social climbing and manœuvring. In power, he is deemed to have falsified Confucianism for his political purposes, and to have used his numerous and varied 'socialistic' measures, in the field of economic policy, to similar ends. His 'nationalisation of the land' was applied only against his powerful opponents among the landlords; others retained their estates and their position. 'Farm credits', the 'ever-normal granary' plan, the 'stabilisation' plans, the 'mountains and lakes' regulations (engrossing to the state the rights in forests and fisheries formerly enjoyed by the people), the debasement and manipulation of the currency, all these worked against the general interest, swelled the State revenues, and finally provoked a genuine peasant rising, the famous rebellion of the 'Red Eyebrows'.

Wang Mang's downfall was hastened also by another group of economic causes which, in greater or less degree, played a part in the history of all the reigns in the long period under review, before and after Wang Mang. Namely, a trend of foreign relations which drained the country's resources in two ways: expensive and unproductive foreign expeditions and campaigns alternating with the cultivation of a foreign trade which brought in only luxuries for the Court and the upper classes, paid for by the export of valuables, which in their turn were paid for by taxing the necessities of the people (12).

Liu Hsiu, who rebelled successfully against Wang Mang, restored the Later (or Western) Han with the support of one of the groups of powerful clans, the 'Nanyang' group. Thus the new ruler's position depended, even more than that of his predecessors in the Early Han, on complete compromise with the clans or cliques. The clans loyal in the Restoration movement were of course especially favoured, but the existing positions of other groups were also recognised. In the Later Han, the locally powerful clansmen not only increased their social and economic power in their own regions, but more and more entered the bureaucracy, reaching its higher ranks and becoming members of the central government. The appearances are that many of the former differences and contentions between the various clans abated, they joined more and more together, room was found in the scholar-administrator ranks for more and more of their sons and brothers; thus was formed the official class, on a larger scale and in a more fully fused condition. This process was accompanied and evidenced by the institution of the Civil Service Examination system, and the increasing appreciation and elaboration of Confucianism.

The economic interests of the elders in the clan-groups, as landowners, bound them to a rather localised outlook. They were supporters of law and order in their localities, but were glad to leave these duties, and the spoils of office, largely to their sons, brothers or nephews, and to others recruited from outside their own circles. The monarchy, it may be said, relaxed and abandoned the policies on which it had previously relied. These were, on the one hand, the formal and systematic policy of Legalism, which meant the Rule of Law and the suppression of any personalisation of politics; and on the other the contrary policy of rule by 'artifice', the skilful and highly personal exercise of statecraft, largely pragmatic and unprincipled. In place of both of these, it was able to rely on the large middle-class of scholar-officials.

This system, in its prime, may have been a suitable and enlightened one; it surely paid less attention to the economic self-interest of its members than to their social standing and cultural progress. Evidently, however, the system failed because it worked badly in the long run. The failure seems to have been especially marked in relation to its highest and lowest classes. Poverty and discontent, land-hunger and oppression, drove the peasantry to cast in their lot with yet another series of rebel leaders; fresh local and clan-groupings arose in the districts; meanwhile, at the top, the eunuch-ridden Court had become degenerate and ineffective.

Economic and historical studies can shed much light on the first two of these factors. Recent work emphasises the development of a new agricultural zone to the south of the Yellow River, which was to become the 'key economic area' on which the progress and expansion of the next period were largely to depend (13). This factor is naturally stressed by those with mechanistic and materialistic interpretations of history. China's contemporary contact and communication with the Western Regions, Central Asia and India are much more important factors, in the eyes of other interpreters. This last is, of course, a field of inquiry in which European Sinologists have a deep and long-standing interest; Oriental writers have also worked on it, but it may be said that they have added little in this direction (14).

This period is, on the whole, one of the most heavily documented in the entire course of Chinese history—as the number of footnotes herewith may show. Yet there are many blanks and deficiencies, and the existing material has by no means been fully analysed, nor even fully collated, as yet (15).

NOTES TO CHAPTER IX

(1) Good recent studies are Eberhard, *History of China*, 1950 (Chapter VI), and Creel, *Confucius: the Man and the Myth*, 1951.

(2) N. L. Swann, *Han Shu 24: Food and Money in Ancient China*, 1950.
Rhea C. Blue, 'The Argumentation of the Shih Huo chapters . . .', *Harvard Journal of Asiatic Studies*, 1951.

(3) Ku Chieh-kang, 'The Han Provincial System', in *Essays for Dr. Tsai Yuen-pai's 60th Birthday*, 1935.
Li Tzu-kuei, 'The 103 Commanderies of Han', in *Tribute of Yu*, VI, 6, 1936.
Chai Chao-chi, 'Hsien System of the Han', *ibid.*, VI, 1, 1936.
Lau Kan, 'Han Frontier District System', *A.S.*, VIII, 2, 1938; 'Han Censorate', *ibid.*, XVII, 1941.
Hamaguchi Shigekuni, 'Appointment of Han Local Officials', in *Rekishigaku Kenkyu*, XII, 7, 1940.
Kamada Shigeo, in *Han Dai Shi Kenkyu*, 1949.
Sakurai Yoshiro, 'Formation of the Censorate', in *Toyo Gakuho*, XXII, 2–3; 'Han Military Titles', *ibid.*, XXII, 3, 1942; 'The Three Elders in the Han Period', in *Essays for Dr. Kato Shigeru's 60th Birthday*, 1941.
Obata Tatsuo, 'Han Village System', in *To-A Jinbun Gakuho*, I, 4, 1941.

(4) Kato Shigeru, 'Public Finance and Palace Finance', in *Toyo Gakuho*, VIII, 2, and IX, 1, 2, 1937; 'Study of the Budget', in *Shirin*, IV, 4, 1920; 'Tax-system of Ancient China', *Shirin*, XVIII, 2–4, 1933.
Yoshida Torao, *Taxation in the Two Han Dynasties*, 1942.

Huang Chun-mo, 'Tax System of the Two Han', in *Shih Huo*, III, 7, 1936.

Chou Chung-hsi, 'Public Finance in the Western Han', *Shih Huo*, III, 8, 1936.

Ma Fei-po, *Taxation*, cit. supra Chapter VIII, note 14.

(5) Hamaguchi Shigekuni, 'Accession and Succession', in *Toho Gakuho*, XIX, 2, 1946; 'Problems of Labour Service under Ch'in and Han', in *Commemorative Essays for Dr. Ichimura*, 1933; 'Age Limits for Conscription during the Han Period', in *Shigaku Zasshi*, XLVI, 7, 1935; 'The Han General Tso Ta-hsiang and his Subordinates', *ibid.*, XLVII, 12, 1936; 'The Southern and Northern Armies of the Former Han', in *Symposium for Dr. Ikeuchi's 60th Birthday*, 1940; 'The Central Armies of the Han', in *Toho Gakuho*, X, 2, 1939.

Sun Yu-tang, 'Military System of the Western Han', in *A.S.*, V, 1, 1937.

Ho Chang Chun, 'Southern and Northern Armies of the Early Han', *ibid.* (*A.S.*, V, 1, 1937).

Lau Kan, *Military System of the Western Han* (cit. supra Chapter VIII, note 11).

(6) Utsunomiya Kiyoyoshi, 'Tenants and Slaves on Private Estates of the Han Period', in *Toyoshi Kenkyu*, I, 1, 1936; 'Clans and Families in the Han Dynasty', in *Shirin*, XXIV, 2, 1939.

Nishijima Sadao, 'Land Ownership in the Han Period', in *Shigaku Zasshi*, LVIII, 1, 1949.

Nishida Tamotsu, 'Middle-class Property in the Han', in *Symposium for Dr. Kato Shigeru's 60th Birthday*, 1941.

(7) Okazaki Fumio, 'On the Shih Huo chapters of the Han History', in *Shinagaku*, III, 1, 1935.

Sasa Hisashi, 'On Tung Chung-shu's Memorial', in *Bunka*, III, 2, 1936.

Uchida Ginzo, 'Anti-mercantile Policies in the Han', in *Nihon Keiza Shi no Kenkyu*, 1944.

Nishida Tamotsu, 'Anti-mercantile policies of Early Han', in *Rekishi Kyoiku*, VI, 4, 1936.

Kojima Sukema, 'Financial Policies of Wu Ti and his successors', in *Toa Keizai Kenkyu*, IV, 1–2.

Nishida Taiichiro, 'State Landownership, Commerce and Industry in China's Formative Period', in *To-A Jimbun Gakuho*, I, 4, 1941.

Chu Hsi-tsu, 'On Hung Yang's Economic Policy' (with a chronology), *Peking University Sociological Quarterly*, IV, 1–2, 1928.

Chang Chun-ming, 'The Genesis and Meaning of Huan K'uan's Discussion on Salt and Iron', *C.S.P.S.R.*, XVIII, 1934.

(8) Ma Fei-po, *Agriculture*, cit. supra, Chapter VIII, note 14.

Yang Lien-sheng, 'Domestic Industries of Han', in *Shih Huo*, I, 6, 1935.

Yang Chung-i, on 'Irrigation–rotation System (of Han)', in *Shih Huo*, I, 6, 1935.

Ch'en Hsiao-chiang, 'Reply to Mr. Yang Chung-i', in *Shih Huo*, II, 1, 1935; further rejoinder by Mr. Yang Chung-i, *ibid.*, II, 4, 1935.
Tseng Ch'ien, 'Irrigation, Military Colonisation and Land Reclamation, Ch'in and Han', in *Shih Huo*, v, 5, 1937.
Hsu Hung-chieh, 'Land System and Agriculture of Ch'in', *ibid.*, III, 7, 1936.
Oshima Riichi, 'On the Writings of Fan Sheng', in *Toho Gakuho*, Kyoto, XV, 4, 1944.
(9) Ma Fei-po, *Manufactures*, and *Commerce*, loc. cit. supra, Chapter VIII, note 4.
Chu Ching-yuan, 'State Industry in the Han Period', *Shih Huo* I, 2, 1935.
(10) Kato Shigeru, 'Monetary System of the First Part of Western Han (with special reference to the "four-string cash")', in *Symposium for Prof. Yamashita's 60th Birthday*, 1938; 'Date of the three-string cash', in *Shigaku Zasshi*, XLIII, 6, 1932.
Ma Fei-po, *Money*, loc. cit. supra, Chapter VIII, note 4.
Han Ke-shin, 'Money System of the Han', in *Shih Huo*, I, 12, 1935.
Tang Hsiao-fei, *Evolution of the Ch'in and Han Monetary Systems, and their Theoretical Basis.*
(11) Makino Tatsumi, *Shina Kazoku Kenkyu*, 1944; *Chukoku Shuzoku Kenkyu*, 1949.
Moriya Mitsuo, 'Hypotheses on Family Structures of the Han Period', in *Shigaku Zasshi*, LII, 6, 1941; 'Clan Aggregation in the Han Period', in *To-A Ronso*, v, 1941.
Nishida Taiichiro, 'Slaves in Western Han', in *Shinagaku*, IX, 4, 1941.
Hamaguchi Shigekuni, 'Forced Labour under the Han', in *Toho Gakuho*, XXIII, 2, 1945.
Lau Kan, 'Slavery during the Han', *A.S.*, v, 1, 1935.
Wu Ching-chao, 'Slavery of Western Han', in *Shih Huo*, II, 6, 1935.
Ma Fei-po, *Slavery*, loc. cit. supra, Chapter VIII, note 4.
Wilbur, M. C., *Slavery in China during the Former Han Dynasty*, Field Museum Series, Chicago, 1943.
(12) Sung I-chen, 'Wang Mang's Reforms' (unfinished article), in *Shih Huo*, v, 2, 1937.
Hu Shih, in *Collected Works*, II, 1930; 'Wang Mang, the Socialist Emperor', in *Journal of North China Branch of R.A.S.*, LIX, 1928.
Franke, O., 'Staatssozialistischer Versuch im alten China', *Berichte der Preussischen Akademie* . . . XIII, 1931 (Chinese translation, of economic portions, in *Shih Huo*, III, 6, 1936; Japanese translation by Uchida in *Shina Kenkyu*, XXX, 1936).
Dubs, H. H., 'Wang Mang and his Economic Reforms', in *T'oung Pao*, XXXV, 1940.
(13) Kuwabara Shitsuzo, 'North and South China from an Historical Point of View', in *Toyo Bunmeishi Ronso*, 1933.
Wada Kiyoshi, 'Historical View of the Development of the Chinese Race', in *Toyoshi Koza*, 1926.

Lau Kan, 'Census Returns and the Geography of the Han Period', in *A.S.*, v, 2, 1934; 'Area and Population Surveys under the Two Han', in *ibid.*

Tao Yuan-chen, 'Southward Migration of the Northern Han', in *Shih Huo*, IV, 11, 1936.

Chao-ting Chi, op. cit. supra, Chapter II, note 24.

(14) Kuwabara Shitsuzo, *Tosei Kotsu Shi Ron* (History of Communications between East and West), 1933.

Shiratori Kurakichi, *Seijo Shi no Kenkyu* (History of the Western Regions), 1941.

Fujita Toyohachi, *Tosei Kotsu Shi Kenkyu*, section on Western Region, 1933.

Miyazaki Ichisada, 'Persia, Rome and the West', in *Shirin*, XXIV, 1, 1939.

Haneda Toru, *Seijo Bunka Shi*, 1948.

Hirth, F., *China and the Roman Orient*, Shanghai, 1885.

Yule, Sir H., *Cathay and the Way Thither*, 1913.

Herrmann, A., *Die alte Seidenstrassen zwischen China und Syrien*, 1916 (Japanese translation by Yasutake Noji, 1944); *Verkehrswege zwischen China, Indien und Rom*, Leipzig, 1922; *Loulan, China, Indien und Rom . . .*, Leipzig, 1931; *Das Land der Seide und Tibet . . .*, Leipzig, 1939.

Sykes, Sir P., *The Quest for Cathay*, 1936.

Teggart, F. J., *Rom und China*, University of California Press, 1939 (Japanese translation by Yamazaki, 1944).

(15) Further bibliography, to end of Han Period:

Anderson, J. G., 'An Early Chinese Culture', *Bulletin of Geol. Survey of China*, v, 1923 (Japanese translation by Mitsumori, 1941); 'Der Weg über die Steppen', *Bulletin of F. E. Museum*, Stockholm, 1, 1929.

Ch'i Ssu Ho, 'Institutions of the Warring States Period', in *Yenching Bulletin*, XXIV, 1938.

Chou Shou-chang, *Additional Annotations to the Later Han History*, 8 vols., 1882; *Supplementary Annotations* to same, 56 vols., 1902.

Chou Chung-hsi, 'Public Finance System of the Han', in *Shih Huo*, III, 8, 1936.

Chu Chung-yung, *Collected Ancient Seals*, 17 vols., 1874.

Chu Ching-yuan, 'Government Industries in the Han Period', in *Shih Huo*, I, 2, 1935; articles on 'House Guests', *ibid.*, II, 11, 1935, and v, 6, 1937.

Egami Namio, *Yurajia Kodai Bunka* (Ancient Culture of Eurasia), 1949; *Ajia Minzoku to Bunka*, 1948.

Hamaguchi Shigekuni, 'Military dispositions at the end of the Later Han', in *Tokyo Toho Gakuho*, XI, 1, 1940.

Hashimoto Masukichi, 'Feudal Sytem of Ancient China', in *Chukoku Bunka Shi Kenkyu*, 1948.

Hirth, F., *Ancient History of China* (to end of Chou), N.Y., 1923.

Kato Shigeru, 'North and South China in Economic History', in *Shakai Keizai Shigaku*, XII, 11–12, 1943.

Kotake Fumio, Articles on Social and Economic Development of Ancient China, in *Shina Kenkyu*, XXXV, 1935.

Kobayashi Noboru, 'Revised Views on Kuan Tzu', in *Rekishigaku Kenkyu*, IV, 6, 1935.

Maeda Naosuke, 'The End of Antiquity in East Asia', in *Rekishi*, I, 4, 1937.

Naito Torajiro, *Chukoku Chuko no Bunka* (Culture of China's Mid-Antiquity), 1947; *Shina Joko Shi* (China's Early Antiquity), 1944.

Niida Noboru, 'Private property in Land in Ancient China and Japan', in *Kokka Gakukai Zasshi*, XLIII–XLIV, 1929–30.

Shida Fudomaro, 'Land tenure and Agrarian Problems', in *Shigaku Zasshi*, XLIII, I, 2, 1932.

Simcox, E. J., *Primitive civilisations*; II. *Land Ownership in China*, N.Y., 1894 (outdated).

Tsuda Sokichi, 'Study of the Chou Kuan', in *Mansen Chiri Shigaku Kenkyu Hokoku*, 1937.

Uchida Ginzo, 'Field System in Ancient Japan', in *Nihon Keizai Shi no Kenkyu*, 1944.

CHAPTER X

CHINA AND ASIA IN THE MIDDLE AGES

After the Han Dynasty, the formative period of Chinese civilisation appears to have been completed, and a long cycle begins in which the pattern appears to be settled and lasting. The conception of the 'Middle Kingdom' acquired a new significance. It indicated that China had evolved a distinctive and self-reliant economy and culture, which was dominant (even domineering) in its own region of the world. The older, and originally greater, culture of India declined; so also did the cultures and the Empires of Central Asia. Once great in their own vigour, and cross-fertilised by Greek and Roman influences, the latter sank in this period in ruins in the desert sands.

In the Han Dynasty, the centre of gravity was still to the westward of China. North, east and south of China, all was primitive darkness. The Han moved at first in the direction of a pan-Asian development; westward across the great land mass, even to a contact with Europe. But it developed also the individuality, the prosperity and metropolitanism of China proper.

In the succeeding period (A.D. 220–580: the Three Kingdoms, Western Chin, Northern and Southern Dynasties) this complex broke up, in a struggle between the Central Country and its own peripheral districts. The Sui Dynasty (580–618) represented a regrouping of the Central Country, and the reassertion of its authority over its surrounding groups. The fine flower of the cultural and political Empire of the T'ang Dynasty (618–906) represented a recrudescence of the spirit and the achievements of the Han: a great revival of the distinctive Chinese culture, economy and polity, and the renewed development of its links with Central and South-eastern Asia.

But, by the time of the T'ang, the centre of gravity was less markedly to China's west. Islam had arisen, to drive a broad wedge between Europe and Asia, and to develop Western

Asia, or the Near East, as an entity of its own. And the areas to the east and south of the Middle Kingdom, the then China proper, were acquiring greater 'weight' in the equilibrium. The T'ang thoroughly incorporated all that we know today as South China; and its influence overflowed to the east, to participate in the creation of the Japanese state and civilisation, and to the south-east, to engender those of what is now Indo-China, and influence those of Siam.

The decline of T'ang was followed by the rise of the Mongols, from the north and north-west of China. They established another—and, until the Japanese venture of 1941–5 and the present effort of the Russians, the last—pan-Asian, and even Eurasian, Empire. But—like the Russian advance today—their movement was not cultural and syncretic, so much as domineering, materialistic, strategic and administrative. They incorporated China, and its borderlands, as one federated unit in their pan-Asian complex.

Typical was what Marco Polo saw and experienced: he was himself enlisted as an administrator in China under the Great Khan, along with other handymen, technicians, merchants, military men and others from all races and all parts of Asia, and even Europe. The Mongols tried to bring Japan also into this cosmopolitan Empire; it was when their invasion failed that Japan first launched out on a strongly separatist and nationalistic path. When the Mongol Empire collapsed, it was natural that China should react also to a strongly nationalistic and self-based attitude. Even the minor border districts tended to the same reaction; notably the Manchus, who in due course attempted the succession to the Mongols, not only in the Gobi regions, but in China proper.

Because of all this, and also because the cultural and practical experience of China represents in the history of Asia very much what that of Greece and Rome represent in the history of Europe, Asian history centres, especially in regard to the period now in question, to a large (but not exclusive) extent on the history of China. At least, the history of China in this period is one of the keys to the understanding of all Asian history, and of Asia's relation to the rest of the world. In these matters the cultural and political aspects have been comparatively much studied, and are relatively well understood; but the economic aspects, which are essential for an understanding of the social implications and the actual livelihood-pattern, have been comparatively neglected.

Advocates of 'pan-Asian' ideas or programmes, of one kind or another, have been widely at work in this field. Some would have all Asia regarded as one unit, from the overlapping points of view of economic, social and cultural considerations. Others would distinguish or subdivide, within this larger cohesion, various other groupings: e.g. China, Japan and Korea as one; South Asia as another, Western and Central Asia as another. Is 'Asia' a 'region' or an entity in the world economically, socially or culturally, in the sense that 'Europe' is, or 'the Occident' in general? Political propagandists of Asian unity usually have the preconceived idea that such is the case, and proceed to elaborate the necessary sentimental and logical reasons afterwards. They are often aided, deliberately or not, by various types of analysts who seek always a comprehensive formula, or set of formulae, and cannot accept a partial or composite explanation. Examples of such, already referred to above, are the theories about the distinctive 'Asiatic mode of production' in ancient times, and the theory of 'universal class struggle', holding that the same fundamental factors are decisive always and everywhere.

Studies in Asian history are really not sufficiently advanced, in any case, for the production of any satisfactory formulae of such a general kind (1). An Oriental Weber, Sombart or Spengler can hardly yet emerge; the data are insufficient, and the sifting process has yet far to go before any satisfactory general theories, of such kinds, can be produced. The existing efforts in that direction lean the more heavily on imagination and dogmatic assertion, the more they attempt to be comprehensive and definite.

In the middle ground there are a large number of historians who are 'eclectics', in the sense that they borrow from more than one of the formula-seeking groups. This makes at times for some strange associations of intellectual 'bed-fellows', and strange political alliances. Numerous and vivid examples of such were given in Japan during the modern Militarist period, when the ultra-Left and the ultra-Right were on common ground, to quite an astonishing extent, in their theories and formulations about 'Asianism' (2). In other countries also, however, the unholy alliance of Marxism with ultra-nationalism is nowadays a familiar phenomenon.

Only a minority of thinkers take the cautious and balanced view that it is not yet possible to reach such sweeping or pretentious conclusions, from the material yet available, or the work that has been done upon it (3). But there is a wide measure of agreement that the economic and social history of China is the matrix, or it may be more appropriate to say the core round which Asian (i.e. at any rate East Asian) history is formed. The only local development which is historically comparable, in formative significance, is that of Japan—which however is obviously, in large part, derivative from China.

The above is necessarily expressed in very general terms, but it may serve to give the student an idea of the basic questions that are raised, at this stage of the study. More concretely, the debate has recently centred on the question of defining 'what were the Middle Ages in China?' To what type of society does the term refer? And to what period does it date? The underlying issue is the meaning, in this case, of the loose description 'medieval', and of that still more loosely applied term 'feudal'.

In the case of European history—and also in that of the history of Japan—fairly precise and significant dates can be set for the 'medieval' era, and a certain type of society can be fairly specifically defined for it. In the case of China, the matter cannot be thus defined or delimited. As suggested in the foregoing, China attained—by the time of the Han Dynasty—a distinctive civilisation of its own, a complete and essentially self-sufficient culture and society of its own, and a position of centrality, a metropolitan situation in its own quarter of the globe. China is deemed to have continued on this basis for as long as thirteen centuries thereafter. There was much evolutionary change, in all this time, and many strong disturbances from within and without; but the system held all the while, fundamentally unimpaired, retaining its confidence, its poise, and its inclination to take a long-term view. These qualities still persist, in substance, and have been carried over in the national inheritance for the future, even through the deep crises of the recent past and the present.

Marxism is obliged to construe all this as one great long interim period. It must assert that substantial progress begins only with its own contemporary revolution. Until then, it must allege, the people were from beginning to end relentlessly suppressed, utterly exploited and shamefully degraded. It cannot tolerate the faintest suggestion that its own vaunted liberation represents only a change from one imperfect political system to another, which may be better, but is still somewhere short of perfection. All or nothing: the change must be from deepest hell to highest Heaven, in one leap. Similarly, it cannot for one moment be admitted that any other systems, the remotest alternatives as well as the immediate opponents of Communism, have any virtues at all. It is almost as treasonable, for instance, to suggest that Britain is socialistic as to say that Generalissimo Chiang is a patriot.

But it is equally treasonable to suggest that anti-Communists go only one stage back in their reactionary propensities; they must be depicted, not merely as stopping the tide today, but as harking back to the darkest and most distant stages of history, and as hankering positively to reintroduce the worst features of those dark ages. Hence the blackening of all previous history is an essential rule; and 'feudalism' (etc.) must be represented as prevailing right down to our own times. The result is that a major part of Chinese history in particular, and Oriental history in general is left a large blank, loosely described as the 'Middle Ages', or 'Feudal period', in which liberated scholars are allowed to fill in only the black spots (4).

The Marxists' highly intellectual-sounding, pseudo-analytical stuff about opposing forces—a Thesis and an Antithesis, leading in each age to a new Synthesis—is essentially at variance with the political requirement just mentioned. But on any practical plane, the latter strongly prevails, and sweeps aside the former.

Some 'bourgeois' views tend, however, to a similarly negative result—though they are not motivated by the same maliciousness. Regrettably, this criticism can be applied to some extent to the bulk of nationalistic Chinese work in this field. Basically, its conception would be of two tremendous eras in Chinese history—an early formative period, in which this magnificent and unique civilisation took shape, and a recent period when it became at last aware of its quality and strength, and took the path of National Resurgence and further development. This tends also to the 'depreciation' of at least 1,000 years of intervening time.

* * *

For these reasons—at the point where the present survey has reached (Chapter IX) the close of the Great Han period—it is here suggested that studies, in relation to the whole subsequent period, can gain clarity and cogency only when much work and thought have been given to two questions of basic perspective. One is, the historic and functional relation of China to the rest of Asia. A fair amount of work has been done in this field, as indicated in preceding chapters; a few more bibliographical references are added here (5). The second perspective question is, the definition and delimitation of the 'Middle Ages'.

The latter issue has been more critically and rather more thoroughly considered in Japan than in China or the West. Miyazaki Ichisada's recent work on this subject has been influential, and is stimulating (6). It involves a studied comparison with European and world-wide history. He places China's Middle Ages between the Three Kingdoms period (220–265) and the end of T'ang. Broadly speaking the preceding period would in his view be classical and antiquarian; the period Three Kingdoms to T'ang would correspond to the resettlement and the cult of social equilibrium which characterised the Middle Ages in Europe; and succeeding periods would see developments in the Far East analogous to those of the Early Modern period in Europe, the rise of nation-states, etc.

There is some consensus of opinion that the end of the T'ang Dynasty is a convenient dividing line. But many different views are expressed. One is that no such delimitations can be convincingly made; because there are great differences between localities, and much overlapping of stages of development (7). Many who know China will agree that this is a necessary warning; conditions in one locality or one time may be quite different from those at another place or date.

Utsunomiya Kiyoyoshi has dated the Middle Ages as extending from the Ch'in and Han periods to the Sui and T'ang (8). But he subdivides this into three 'characteristic' periods: (i) the Ch'in and Han, which saw the completion of the Ancient Society, (ii) the Six Dynasties, an 'autonomous' period (jiritsuteki—it 'ganged its ain gait'), (iii) the Sui and T'ang, which combined the 'political' (well-ordered) and 'autonomous' tendencies in a new consolidation. (On the last point, it should be explained that a forced or 'dialectical' reunion is envisaged, rather than an ideal harmonisation.)

Maeda Naosuke (9) has an extensive, though rather vague, criticism of the above views, but refers to some interesting details of economic history. With other Japanese writers, he notes that large holdings of land may arise without widespread dispossession of farmers, and that the large landownership of Han times may have been quite different from that of the T'ang period. He discusses further such points as the following:

Before the T'ang era, 'slaves' or 'servants' generally provided the labour in China; the exact meaning of the former term, especially, is uncertain, but it must indicate some form of 'serfdom'. From the end of the T'ang onwards, by contrast, the cultivators appear in the main to be 'tenants'. Dr. Miyazaki interprets the matter as follows: in the Wei, Chin and Northern and Southern Dynasties the 'clans' rewarded their own loyal followers with tenancies on comparatively 'free' conditions, while holding other types of persons such as prisoners, and the descendants of the 'slaves' of the preceding period, as serfs. But the terms in question (10) are far from clear in their etymology and application.

These are only a few examples of the disputed problems arising in respect of this period. The whole development, from the end of the Han to that of the T'ang, is an extremly complicated matter. Many new factors come into play, and many new aspects have to be considered, when we come to this stage of Chinese history. One question is that of the development of the monetary system. The traditional view, of the older generation of historians, has been that the use of money declined during the Wei, Western Chin and Northern and Southern periods; this view is now questioned. It is held that barter may have increased, but that the money system did not break down.

The period after the Han is also that of the first major development of Southern China, from the economic and social point of view. The basic pattern of the Chinese livelihood was altered from that time, with a much greater emphasis on rice as a staple crop. This necessitated new forms of administration, and led to new ideas and methods of land reform. New clan-groupings and class-relationships arose.

From the point of view of improving our knowledge and handling of Chinese history in respect of this period, in the economic aspect particularly, two ways seem therefore to be open. One is to work 'from the ground up' to accumulate more detailed evidence, and sift it ever more carefully; thus to proceed gradually from the particular to the general, until a broad characterisation of the specific nature of Chinese history is established. The other is the opposite procedure: to try to settle the general principles from an *a priori* point of view, to focus ideas within a certain logical and coherent perspective, before attempting to fill in the details. Neither approach seems to have had any marked success as yet.

For the former, the amount of detail is excessive in total, yet is most unevenly distributed—on many key points, the amount of evidence is insufficient. The latter type of approach, the macrocosmic view, requires more detachment from personal, racial or political attitudes than it has yet been possible to expect in the Orient (or for that matter in the Occident, as far as the latter's views on the Orient are concerned); a long and thorough apprenticeship in historical work is essential, in the province of Oriental history, besides a deeper cultivation of abstract detachment, before the necessary breadth of judgment can be attained. In this situation, the dogmatism of some of the prevailing schools is ridiculously inappropriate; far from our understanding of all this history being complete, it is only just at its beginning.

NOTES TO CHAPTER X

(1) Nakayama Hachiro, in . . . *Shiori* (op. cit. Chapter II, note 11), IV, pt. 2, Chapter 1.

(2) A well-known example is the popular and influential Moriya Katsumi's *Toyo-teki Seikatsu-ken* (The Oriental Lebensraum), 1942, which expounded the Marxian 'Asian system of production' in terms fully acceptable to the avowedly militarist and fascist factions.

(3) Eminent Japanese scholars like Miyazaki Ichisada have on the other hand maintained a reserved attitude. His *General Study of Asian History*, 1947, cit. supra Chapter V, note (8), is an excellent survey of 'types of Asian history', related to the general background of World History. The same writer's *Toyoteki Sekai*, 1950, appears at first sight to be a summary and dogmatic work, but proves on closer examination to be a well-considered thesis.

Egami Namio's *Asian Races and Cultures* (see Chapter IX, note (15) above) suggests that each country or portion of Asia must be treated separately; most of the races of Asia have been agricultural, and have developed differently from each other, whereas the nomadic races are supposedly more conservative and have remained a more uniform group.

(4) This is a broad tendency, within which there are significant variations. Communist 'double-talk' seeks in this respect, as in others, 'to have it both ways'. The crude vilification of the past has been a strong feature of their propaganda in China generally—but more especially on the level of 'popular' material, for the masses. 'Intellectual circles' in China are allowed to be more discriminating at times, even in Party discussions. In the Soviet Union proper, a noticeably wider interpretation is allowed. For example, the relevant sections of that monumental Soviet work of reference, the *Bolshaya Sovietskaya Entsyklopedia*, state that the medieval period in China came more or less to an end with the T'ang; though generally, in Japan, the official Soviet conception is regarded as agreeing rather with that of Naito than that of Miyazaki.

(5) Aoki Tomitaro, *Toyogaku no Seiritsu to sono Hatten*, 1940 (astonishingly, this work deals ably with Western and Japanese work, but omits all Chinese work on the subject!); 'Post-war Asian Studies in Europe and America', in *Sekai no Shakaikagaku*, 1948.

Ch'ueh T'ung-tsu, 1937 (Japanese translation by Kotake and Kojima, same title, 1942).

Kotake Fumio, 'Essay on Economic and Social Development of China in the Mid-Medieval Period', in *Shina Kenkyu*, 1935.

Latourette, K. S., *Short History of the Far East*, 1946; *The Chinese, their History and Culture* (2nd ed., 1938, translated into Japanese by Okazaki Saburo, as *Shina no Rekishi to Bunka*, 3 vols., 1939–41), 3rd ed., 1946.

Moriya Katsumi, *Toyoteki Shakai no Rekishi to Shiso*, 1948.
Sugimoto Naojiro, 'On the Periods of Oriental History', in Hiroshima Bunrika University's symposium, *Toyo no Gensei yori mitaru Shi-teki Ronso*, 1935.
Teng Chih-ch'eng, 1934.
To-A Kenkyujo (ed.), *Iminzoku no Shina-toji* (Rule of Alien Peoples in China), 1943.
Zen-Ajia Rekishi Taikei, 1939.

(6) See note (3) above.

(7) Sugimoto Naojiro, op. cit. note (5) above.
Naka Michiyo, *Toyo Shigaku*, 1948.
Kuwabara Shitsuzo, '. . . Southward Development of China', in *Toyoshi Setsu-en*, 1927; and op. cit. supra, Chapter IX, note (13).

(8) Utsunomiya Kiyoyoshi, 'The Domain of Oriental History', in *Toko*, II, 1947.

(9) Maeda Naosuke, op. cit. supra, Chapter IX, note (15).

(10) On these interpretations, and on many other points, Mr. Maeda's ideas are widely disputed in Japan, especially by the Kyoto school.

CHAPTER XI

THE MEANING OF THE 'MIDDLE AGES'

The last chapter reviewed some of the difficulties encountered in defining what were 'the Middle Ages' in the history of China. The interpretation differs according to whether China is taken as an entity in itself, or in association with some more general 'Asian' complex. In either case the difficulties of classification are interesting in themselves, and give rise to fruitful discussions. When all is said and done, however, another very large question poses itself. Is not the term 'Middle Ages' or Medieval period itself a complete misnomer in this case? Does it not represent an entirely false analogy with other parts of the world, with societies which are structurally and generically different?

The expression 'Middle Ages' represents inherently a residual classification. Two periods of history are indicated by the speaker or writer, and presented in sharp focus. An ancient epoch is taken as the starting point (with 'classical' attributes); and a Modern Era as the culminating phase, in which mankind has reached the summit of progress, or come at least in clear sight of it. The interim between these two terms of reference is pictured as a vague and protracted 'middle' period of floundering or uncertain delay, during which the 'progressive' tendencies (i.e. those which in retrospect seem to have favoured the development of modern features) struggle, often vainly, though at long last successfully, against other forces (retrospectively labelled as 'reactionary').

Without going far into the general philosophy of history, it must be remarked that all such contradistinctions are relative and arbitrary. Only in a rare minority of instances can any very definite dividing lines be drawn. Rarely does a given period appear as an absolute, a clear and complete base-period, unmistakably either the starting-point or the completing phase of any identifiable cycle or stage in evolutionary development. Such instances are especially rare in the case of the history of China, in which several 'classical' or 'base' periods may be distinguished, alternatively or in some concatenation with each other. None of them leads to any very specific denouement or outcome-stage of its own; but each contributes to the long record of many 'waves' of varied influences, protractedly and complicatedly overlapping each other. It is possible to establish fairly convincingly some rhythmic or cyclical patterns in all this, but not to prove, with anything like equal conviction, that it all works out in some definite long-term trend, from state A to state B.

The basic Marxist conception of a crude social dynamics, with an absolute A passing into an absolute B, as the result of a distinctive Thesis clashing with an identifiable Antithesis to create a new Synthesis, is absurd and irrelevant in this Asian context generally, and in the case of China in particular. Historians of the future may observe with compassion how many people in the Far East in our own day were so long and so deeply affected by a particular inference and some special terminology, drawn from a study of the development of a particular area (Western Europe) during a certain period (the thirteenth to the nineteenth centuries of the Christian era).

For that particular period and area may furnish one of those instances described above as being in the minority, from the point of view of the wide range of historical cases available to us. Western Europe did emerge, from the heritage of Rome passing through the melting-pot of the Dark Ages, into a well-definable, characteristic, unitary type of society, accurately describable in terms of 'Medievalism', 'Feudalism', etc. It had a common, coherent, consistent, universal and explicit outlook, pattern, way of life, etc., known and clear to us, which in this case may appropriately be called the Middle Ages. In the next identifiable stage, it passed through the decay of that society and the break-up of its equilibrium, to the rise—from the evolutionary development of features intrinsic to itself—of a new state of society. The latter in its turn is well-definable, characteristic, unitary, common, universal and explicit in the area; namely, capitalism and democracy, in the Western meaning of those terms.

Asia in general, and China in particular, have not in the corresponding period any such clear base-form to begin with or completion-form to end with; and accordingly have no intervening middle period which can possibly be construed as a transition between the one and the other. The modern age came in China, and most other parts of Asia, as something alien in nature, imposed from without; in Europe it was an indigenous development.

The information about China (and other parts of Asia) is actually too scanty, and has been as yet too little sifted, for us to venture dogmatically to lay down finalised representations of any of the 'classical' or basically formative periods distinguishable in Chinese history (such as the Confucian, Han or T'ang eras). Nor is the information a great deal more plentiful or precise in respect of the Modern period, in the case of those areas. At the same time it appears clear that present-day Asia in the main (apart from Japan, and a few smaller centres such as Hongkong) is actually proceeding to evade or omit the phase of state of Western Capitalism altogether, or to experience it only partially and in denatured form.

It is significant that Marx himself did not attempt specifically to force Asia into his theoretical mould for Europe, as, for instance, by postulating that its present evolutionary phase began with 'Feudalism' and ends with Capitalism overthrown by Proletarianism. Marx and Engels were actually content in their earlier historical work (with, perhaps, the cultural arrogance of true nineteenth-century Europeans) to leave Asia generally outside in the darkness, as the domain of 'Asiatic despotism' and 'The Asiatic mode of production'. They added to this however—a theory developed by Lenin—that capitalism in its 'mature' phase of Imperialism would spread all over the world, creating the same general 'antithesis' and the peculiar 'contradictions' of the system, everywhere.

Clearly it was envisaged that this would go on until large and strong proletariats (by which they definitely meant industrial working classes) would be created everywhere, which would overthrow capitalism. The founders of Marxism and Leninism sometimes refer to capitalism and Imperialism, in the meantime, as relatively progressive forces, since these would create a world-economy and world-wide industrialisation. The original Marxism-Leninism tended to regard the former at least, and to a considerable extent also the latter, as inevitable prerequisites for the world revolution. Some of their present-day disciples consider that they would have been horrified to be told that Socialism could be built on peasant riots, or in countries without large industries.

The perspectives of all this are uncertain, but the predictions are in any case not greatly more accurate than their prophecies about Europe, which envisaged the constant impoverishment of the masses, the disappearance of the middle class, etc. These considerations are not directly relevant to the present discussion, but they are necessary, to illustrate how foreign to Asian conditions are all the preconceptions of Marxism. Marxism must always be seen as a whole; its incidental applications to Asian conditions depend very deeply on its essentially European and nineteenth-century origins for their content, and on preconceptions like the above for their form.

* * *

It is at the stage which the present study has reached—the discussion of the centuries which succeeded the Han and preceded the T'ang, the period from about A.D. 220 to 580—that it is deemed suitable to restate a warning against all such formalism in thought, and against the uncritical application of European terms. For it is from this period onwards that very general, inaccurate, sometimes irrelevant use is made of terms like 'medieval' and 'feudal', and of the implied analogies with Europe.

It is better to risk overstressing this feature than to leave it unnoticed. Forewarned is forearmed, from the point of view of the student. Once he has grasped this point, and is on his guard against the use of terms like 'feudal' and 'landlordism' as catchwords, refuses to let assertion stand for proof, and rejects any 'automatic' analogy with European conditions, the study of Chinese history is relieved of much of its one-time formalism; it appears in its true light as a magnificent record of human experience and achievement.

After the Han, the next great age of China was the T'ang. It was noted in the last chapter that this period is widely accounted the 'Middle Ages' of China; Wei, Chin and the Northern and Southern Dynasties being the 'early medieval' phase, and the T'ang the 'late medieval'. Yet the former phase saw many adverse and powerful new factors at work; a number of these were mentioned in the last chapter. The T'ang period in its turn experienced other changes, and felt other new influences. It is hard to understand how this particular interval in history comes to be so readily and widely accepted, not merely as constituting one complete and identifiable cycle in history, or step in social evolution, but as being the one which qualifies for the medieval position—which spans the gulf of time between the 'ancient' and 'modern' eras.

In Japan, the name of Dr. Naito Torajiro has lasting authority. Foreshadowed by some minor writings (1), his major work on this period (2)—the title of which, it may be noted, calls this era not the 'Middle Ages' but the 'Mid-Antiquity' of China—gave a classic modern description of the period, representing it as one of historical decline from the golden age of the Han Emperor Wu. Kotake Fumio (3) drew careful analogies with the European Middle Ages, and suggested a more positive interpretation of the period from the Three Kingdoms to T'ang, in terms of the rise of new and alternative forms of economic and social organisation.

Meanwhile, thought in China (and, through translation, in Japan) was being influenced by such work as that of Wu Hsien-hsiang, a member of T'ao Hsi-sheng's 'Shih Huo' group (4), which tended to emphasise this classification, without extending the range of data covered. His contribution was valuable, for instance, in combating the traditional view that this was a period of such economic retrogression that even money went out of use; but on this evidence it seems to have gone too far in the other direction, in the preconceived Marxian contention that this period was one of evolution to a 'higher' historical stage.

For this period, the data on such subjects as land (ownership and use), taxation and labour service are more abundant than those on such aspects as trade, handicrafts or manufacture; though it is true that the latter have not been so fully studied as the former.

Another modern Japanese historian, Dr. Okazaki Fumio, is accounted a pioneer and a lasting authority on this period (5). Another Japanese writer, whose contribution is recognised as of major importance in the category of general treatises on this period, is Shida Fudomaro (6).

The Marxist schools have made enthusiastic use of a suggestion from another direction. Namely, the explanation of this period in terms of the effects of the contemporary opening-up of South China. Chi Chao-ting's *Key Economic Areas* (7) is a basic reference in this connection; though, in fact, it may represent essentially a type of geographical or 'mechanistic' determinism, which may really be at variance with the Marxists' own type of social determinism. The work of leading Japanese commentators on this aspect may give varied and important clarifications.

Kuwabara (8) stresses 'cultural' factors more than the economic ones. Kato (9) deals especially with technical or industrial changes. Okazaki analyses, on the one hand (10), the spread and increase of rice-cultivation. He notes the gradually increasing importance of rice in North China, from ancient times to the Wei-Chin period. In the Later Han period, he notes, the Government greatly encouraged rice-production, and the Chinese liking for rice increased so much that it became henceforth the principal grain. In the Wei, particularly, rice-cultivation played in his view an important part in the military colonisation or 'barrack-field' policies.

On the other hand (11), Okazaki deals with the 'powerful clans' aspect of this period; he sees the local groups gaining power especially in the south, joined by refugees or emigrants from the north, and opposing other groups in or around the capital.

Another aspect is, however, involved in this general question. It appears that not only clansmen, but farmers and other types of emigrants moved in this troubled period from the north into the south. After the end of Eastern Chin, there was an interesting development. A policy of 'Land Reform' (called by the same name as is applied in Communist China today) (12) was enforced, and the immigrants were classified and registered in certain categories (13). As a result of this, and of other factors, the whole system of local and provincial government was greatly changed in this period.

In this period, new bases of class-distinction were evolved. It does not seem, however, that any important classes went out of existence in the period, or declined to any great extent; nor was it that a new class emerged, destined to be the next ruling class. The new class-distinctions seem to have meant little or nothing more than a rearrangement of the existing classes in the social scale.

New institutions or policies were nevertheless devised, to meet the complex and ever-changing situation. Some of these were improvisations, some adaptations of the traditions and usages of preceding periods in China; others were actual importations from foreign lands and alien tribes or peoples. Usually, there was some fusion of all these elements. In this case therefore (in contra-distinction to the basically unchanged class-structure) it seems that there were distinct governmental and institutional innovations, not merely a reshuffling of old arrangements under new names. Meanwhile, China was constantly ravaged and shaken by disorder within, and attacks from outside barbarians.

If the view taken in the last two paragraphs is correct, this period in China appears completely different from the Medieval period in Europe, in at least three essential respects: namely, that (*a*) the class-structure appears comparatively rigid, while (*b*) the governmental and institutional structure varied, but (*c*) the variations are largely attributable to 'external' factors (invasions, frontier shifts, etc.). In the case of early Medieval Europe, (*a*) class-relationships changed but (*b*) the institutional framework resisted change, and (*c*) the changes are ascribable to interior and local forces, rather than those intruding from outside. The conditions in China would seem to resemble those of the 'Dark Ages', rather than the 'Middle Ages' of Europe. The so-called 'Dark Ages' were the period when the fall of Rome was followed by extremely unstable conditions of political and social life, attended by great migrations of tribes and peoples, out of which arose a new and firm system of military feudalism. The Middle Ages of Europe are broadly envisaged as the later period, in which feudalism broke down and was replaced eventually by bourgeois, capitalistic and nationalistic forms of society.

There are some advantages in applying the description 'Middle Ages' to this whole period in China. The term is conveniently vivid. There are some valid comparisons to be made with Medieval Europe. But this appellation is on the whole dangerous; especially if 'Medieval' is taken, not as a comparison, but as a definition.

In the last two chapters we have, however, reviewed the analytical difficulties, in respect of his period, in a manner essentially negative. In the next two chapters, an attempt will be made to show positively what were the economic and social characteristics of this period and that of the T'ang. From this more positive approach, some suggestions for a better description or classification may emerge. Meanwhile, the existing literature on the subject may be regarded with some caution, in so far as the terminology, and the comparisons or assimilations which it implies with European models, may be misleading.

NOTES TO CHAPTER XI

(1) Naito, 'Outline of the T'ang and Sung Periods', in *Rekishi to Chiri*, IX, 5; also in *Toyo Bunka Shi*, 1923.

(2) *Culture of China's Mid-Antiquity*, op. cit. Chapter IX, note (15), 1947. This volume consists of his last lectures at Kyoto Imperial University.

(3) Kotake, op. cit. Chapter X, note (5).

(4) Wu Hsien-hsiang, 1936. Japanese translation by Utsunomiya Kiyoyoshi and Masumura Hiroshi, 1939, contains in addition a very useful bibliography of Chinese and Japanese works.

(5) Okazaki, *Nam-bei Cho ni okeru Shakai-Keizai Seido*, 1939; *General History of Liao, Tsin, etc.* (Pt. I, Economy and Finance; Pt. II, The Social System), 1932.

(6) Shida, 'Oriental Medieval History', in *Sekai Rekishi Taikei* (Heibonsha), 1941.

(7) Chi, *Key Economic Areas*, cit. supra, Chapter II, note (4).

(8) Kuwabara Shitsuzo, 'North and South China', cit. supra. Chapter IX, note (13), also in *Essays for Dr. Shiratori's 60th Birthday*; 'Southward Movement . . .', cit. supra. Chapter X, note (7).

(9) Kato Shigeru: See Chapter IX, note (15); 'N. and S. China from the point of view of Economic History', in *Shakai Keizai Shigaku*, XII, 11–12, March 1943, reprinted in *Shinagaku Zasso*, 1944.

(10) Okazaki Fumio: the first work cited in note (5) above.
(11) *Ibid.*, study of the successive State Capitals in and around Nanking, from Wu of the Three Kingdoms, through the Six Dynasties.
(13) Inaba Iwakichi, 'Land Reform and Group-Organisation in the Year of the Golden Dog', in *To-A Keizai Kenkyu*, XVII, 1, 1933.

CHAPTER XII

FROM HAN TO T'ANG: CHINESE SOCIETY IN THE THIRD TO THE SIXTH CENTURIES

The Han Empire produced a firm and lasting basis for the subsequent political and social development of China, in the form of what has been called 'the Gentry-State'. A class, supposedly independent and enlightened—chosen through the celebrated Examination System on the basis of scholastic selection alone, as a Civil Service into which anyone of ability might enter, whatever his social origin—was set up to fulfil the administrative functions.

This class degenerated into a condition of cliquishness and intrigue; and its members, individually or in groups and coteries, became variously involved or absorbed in the strife of vested interests (especially in landownership which was the main criterion of economic power) and in the rivalries of clans, families, localities and associations. At the same time, the life of the Court and the Metropolis degenerated into a condition of complete corruption, and came to be dominated by the Eunuchs. A third factor was the rise of the provincial generals, who became rulers of great areas and leaders of powerful armies, like the War Lords of modern times. There was still a fourth factor, which played perhaps a lesser part: namely, the rise of turbulent movements of resistance among the common people of the lower classes.

The popular movements in the last-mentioned category are clearly associated with the conditions of agrarian discontent. For expression they turned largely to Taoism. The philosophy of Lao Tze had become an organised religion, degenerating into a vulgar and superstitious cult of popular magic. Its priests and high priests, in whose ranks were found many political adventurers, were magicians or sorcerers (shamans). Their greatest effort was the rebellion of the Yellow Turbans (from A.D. 184). It was defeated, and the generals became the main factors in the situation; among them, the foremost was

Ts'ao Ts'ao, who relied to a great extent on his Hsiung Nu soldiers, the Hun tribesmen whom he had permitted and encouraged to settle in Shansi and other areas of North China. Ts'ao Ts'ao's son founded (in 220) a new dynasty, the Wei, and this event marks the final downfall of the Han.

The succeeding period, of more than three centuries, is traditionally and conventionally represented in most of the general histories of China as a mere 'phase', or something of an interlude. In view of the duration and the complexity of this period, it is difficult to accept such an interpretation. This large slice of history, with all the involved and diverse strains of development that it contained, must rank as a formative period in its own right. For reasons discussed in the last chapter, it may be very misleading to call it one of 'transition'.

The political changes, and the very multiplicity of names, are extremely difficult to follow, or to present accurately in any brief summary. The underlying fact is that China was split into two main regions, Northern and Southern. At first (220–280) there were the Three Kingdoms (Wei, Wu and Shu-Han); briefly reunited under the Western Chin (280–307), only to be disintegrated again, with a general division between North and South. In the North, a score of 'dynasties', being regimes of a more or less tribal character resulting mainly from the incursions of various types of 'Northern Barbarians', can be listed over the next three centuries. In the South there were the 'Six Dynasties' during this period, representing generally the alternation of various 'cliques', but appearing and claiming to be properly 'Chinese': Wu (220–80), Eastern Chin (317–419), Liu-Sung (420–78), Southern Ch'i (479–501), Liang (502–6) and Ch'en (557–87). (Sometimes the last five of these are referred to as 'The Five Dynasties'.)

In the North, the Chinese civilisation in all its aspects was thus mingled with, and greatly influenced by, 'barbarianisms' of various kinds. It seems, however, to be a misrepresentation to say that it was 'swamped' thereby. Whether as a hard core, a firm basis, or a durable residue, there remained a distinctive corpus of Chinese institutions and traditions continuing there, to such an extent that historians tend to think that various degrees of 'assimilation' resulted—which, it is usually suggested, was assimilation of the barbarians by the Chinese, rather than vice versa. Regarding the South, on the other hand, it is a misrepresentation to state that meanwhile the pure and true heritage of China was there handed down unchanged. In the South also, the process was one of much contact and some mingling with barbarians of various kinds. The South was already peopled by various tribes, different of course from those of the Northern and North-western lands, whose influence on the Chinese is also distinctly traceable.

In both cases, therefore, a 'Chinese' economy and society persisted, the continuity of which was fundamentally unbroken, though its stream of development shows some deviations, and many confluences from outside itself. At the end of Chapter X above, it was noted that there are two ways in which historical research might advance towards a clearer understanding of the period. One is by a closer and more detailed examination of the internal facts and workings of the specifically Chinese society of that time, seen (so to speak) 'from within'. The other is the external approach, studying the outside influences and the general environment, as they affected the same society. When these approaches have yielded sufficient information and insight, the results can be combined to give a full and accurate assessment of the period and its setting.

In respect of this as of other periods of Chinese history, Oriental scholars have naturally tended to the 'internal' viewpoint and procedure, while Occidental scholars have naturally tended mainly to the 'external' approach. Here we may briefly survey some of the main or characteristic findings of each group, and see how far they may be combined into a coherent description of the epoch as a whole. Unfortunately, the factual data appear hardly sufficient for the former procedure, of detailed 'internal' study, to have reached much finality as yet; while, under the second heading, though numerous very general treatments have been produced, no thoroughly analytical work has yet become available for this period. Professor Wittfogel has made a full presentation of one later period however (the Liao, 937–1124, another Northern 'dynasty of conquest'), which is intended to be the first in a very long-term programme of similar works, to cover all the significant periods.

In the present chapter, then, a slight (and merely preliminary) introduction is given to some characteristic attempts by contemporary scholars to define the innate and intrinsic character of the Chinese society of the fourth to the sixth centuries, or the resultant of its inherent forces during that period. In the following chapter, the 'external' approach, as exemplified generally by the conclusions of modern scholars in the West, will be reviewed.

* * *

After the end of the Western Chin (265–317), the class distinction between gentry and commoners was drawn more strictly than ever (1). The discrimination appears to have been especially necessary, from the later days of the Han onwards, in the refugee-receiving and emigrant-absorbing areas of China (notably the domains of Wei and Chin). The great migrations, involving chiefly a peasant population, occasioned the collapse of the former administrative system—especially at the purely local level. In the Han period, the local ('autonomous village') system was the main foundation of the social order—or at any rate one of its main pillars. In the Eastern Chin period (317–419) the same nomenclature continued to be used, but evidently the basis of the system had collapsed. The county (hsien) had replaced the village as the basic unit of administration.

It is generally believed that the independent village system devised under the Han checked the acquisition of land by wealthy or powerful individuals, and the consequent reduction of independent peasants to the status of serfs or retainers. When the local government system collapsed, such engrossment of property and subjection of persons became the tendency. The governments of the Wei Dynasty of the Three Kingdoms (220–265) and its successor the Ch'ao (304—352) are considered to have instituted the famous 'barrack-field' or 'camp-field' (2) system, partly as a measure of social policy, to meet this social crisis and give some protection to the peasantry. This is apart from, or in addition to, its function in securing the occupation of newly opened frontier districts and the garrisoning of strategic points generally. The policy in question is that of settling selected places and areas with garrisons of soldier-farmers—soldiers who tilled the soil and provided their own food-supplies, or alternatively peasants trained as first- or second-line reservists, who could be called to the colours at short notice (3).

At about the same time, however, in the northern territory of the Wei particularly, a new system of communal organisation, on the village level, makes its appearance: namely, the 'Three Grades System' (4). This was a new system of census-registration and tax-collection, designed to subserve the county governments. The data on this are very limited, and their interpretation is a subject of dispute among scholars (5).

This problem has to be regarded in close conjunction with that of the progress and influence of the 'locally powerful clans' in this period. Some well-documented studies by Japanese writers give a broadly 'materialistic' view of this subject (6). Another authority drew useful sociological inferences from the general literature and folk-lore of the period (7). Another studied, from the standpoint of legal history, the contemporary conventions and practices relating to marriage, illustrating in another way the strictness of the discrimination between the upper and the lower classes—a corollary of which is the complete absence of any middle class (8).

A striking feature of the period is the low social standing of the warriors or military men. Their status would seem to have worsened, in comparison with preceding periods. It is well known that soldiers have ever since been in low social esteem in China. This is a striking point of contrast between China and Japan. In China the word 'shih' denotes a scholar-gentleman; in Japan the same character is 'samurai', and conveys first and foremost the military significance. Japanese scholars have naturally paid much attention to the point, in relation to this period especially, in view of the fact that in Japan, in contrast to China, a military ruling-class emerged.

Kato Shigeru represents the warrior classes in China as 'humiliated' by the powerful clans, of whom they became mere retainers (9). Hamaguchi Shigekuni traced the social 'segregation' to which they were subjected. He suggests that in the Han period the military and the farming classes were in close harmony and unity, or may even be considered as one and the same class; but that they were separated and estranged in the period now under review (10). The evidence on this matter is of great importance from another point of view also: it proves that the contemporary society was definitely not 'feudal'. A feudal system is one in which the loyalty of subordinates is assured, against the grant of fiefs.

No such compact of moral obligation and allegiance, with or without its material basis of owner-and-tenant relationships, can be said to have prevailed in China in the period now in question. The other ideas which enlarged the social philosophy of the Medieval period in Europe—such as the desire for social equilibrium and security, 'a place for everyone, and everyone in his place', the Common Law and the respect for Equity—were completely lacking. On the exact position of the lower classes—in terms of social estimation, legal rights, or traditional safeguards—there is very little information, for China in this period. (There is more for the next period to be considered, the T'ang.) But the data appear sufficient to show conditions quite different from those European ones from which the conceptions of 'feudal' and 'medieval' so largely derive (11).

The above indicates, in the present writer's view, roughly the extent to which any conclusions are possible from the data so far available, in the direction of defining the general nature of the social system in the pre-T'ang era. Recent progress has perhaps been in the direction of factual and descriptive studies, rather than in the drawing of general conclusions. Agricultural methods and theories of the period have been studied by some competent scholars. The Japanese must again be mentioned in the leading place. For example, the Japanese Ministry of Agriculture was responsible for the production in 1949 of a well-edited reprint of the *Governance of the People*, attributed to Chia Ssu-hsieh of Northern Wei (12).

Some of Okazaki's work deals with the 'barrack-field' system (13). The Ch'ao-Wei Dynasty conscripted people for military service, and gave them certain designated rice-fields to cultivate, in fixed garrison-areas. These fields were selected from the so-called 'official fields'—principally lands which had reverted to government ownership because their previous holders had left them, in times of war and famine. They were under the control of military officers, and paid fixed taxes, the proceeds of which were earmarked for military purposes. In these respects they were in a separate category from the ordinary agricultural lands, the farmers of which were under the control of the civil governors of the hsiens (counties), and were subject to different and variable taxes.

Such was the original system. But the situation became more complex after the Wei period, when the Chin expanded territorially to the south of the Yangtse River and established new systems, known as the 'occupied field', 'assigned field' and 'household allotment' systems. It is widely believed that these devices were largely formal or theoretical—i.e. that they were never applied in practice to any great extent. Nevertheless, they must be studied, as they are essential for an understanding of the aims and principles which governed the conduct of these states and their successors. Moreover, this is the starting-point for an understanding of the 'field-equalisation law' (or 'system' or 'principle') which subsequently became a leading issue, and has great importance not only in the history of China but also in those of Japan, Indo-China and Siam. There are many opinions on the nature of the attempt to prevent or limit the engrossment of land by individual large-scale owners, and to develop systems of communal ownership or equal-sharing, through the succeeding centuries (14).

Miyazaki Ichisada's contribution of 1935, on *The Household Allotment System of the Chin Emperor Wu* (15), startled the scholars. He rejected the traditional acceptance of the Shih Huo chapters of the Chin history, and asserted that a version drawing on general lexicography (t'ung tien) was to be preferred. His hypothesis was that the assigned-field system was a result of the decay of the barrack-field system. The former replaced the latter; as and when the barrack-field system (of military colonisation, and cultivation by the garrisons) broke down, the soldiers were 'assigned' the same fields for their individual use and authority; the general (civil) population were under the 'occupied field law', subject to county and district officials, and regarded perhaps as tenants of State-owned land. He was able to show that the land system of the T'ang derived not only from the field-equalisation of Northern Wei, but also from the Chin and Wei-Ch'ao barrack-field.

Others hold that the barrack-field system did not go out of existence, to be replaced by assigned fields, but that the various systems continued to exist together. There is, however, some consensus of opinion that though the forms and conditions changed very much from place to place and time to time, in this period, the broad tendency was for a large number of farmers to gain increasing independence. The people of the assigned fields (soldiers formerly on barrack-fields, or their descendants) became independent farmers ('yeomen'), others (on 'occupied fields') received better treatment, as tenants under the State. The land was 'nationalised' to this extent and in this sense: that all except a comparatively few rich landlords paid systematic rent (or rather product-taxes or dues) to the State, and that even landlords were subject to the confiscation or reallotment of lands by the State. It is agreed however that this system was very imperfect, if not altogether unsuccessful; it did not prevent the buying up of land by rich men, or the collusion of aristocrats and officials for that purpose (16).

It is not clear what was the nature of the 'tax' or 'levy' (17) on the farmers. Presumably it was primarily a corvée, i.e. compulsory labour-service. On this point, again, there is more evidence in the later period of the T'ang. Some investigators work backwards from the T'ang period, to find the answers for the Chin and Wei. Sogabe Shizuo (18) noted that labour-service was divided into various kinds of grades in the T'ang period, and may have included 'mixed assessments', partly taxes paid in money or kind. In the Chin and the Six Southern Dynasties there were no such distinctions, and probably not in the Twenty Northern Dynasties.

Sogabe postulates that the 'assigned field' was the public land on which some people performed their labour services; these people would be all the male members of every family other than the head or householder, who would be given an 'occupied field', probably larger in area, but would have to pay taxes. This view depends on a particular interpretation of the terms used; but is supported by some facts, e.g. the differentiation between 'adults' and 'juveniles' in the assessment for labour service (19). Thus some writers see the 'occupied' and 'assigned' lands as two different or conflicting categories, while others were able to reconcile the two concepts and see them as parts of a common system (20).

The problem of land-ownership is a very complicated one. Social historians generally are content to regard the system in this period as one of State-ownership, but from the point of view of legal history (as stressed by writers like Niida and Nakada) it is definable as private-ownership under certain statutory limitations. Field-equalisation involved, in any case, a profound change in the conception of ownership; the land reform effected under that name proved more successful, and more lasting, than previous attempts.

Before the Ch'in Dynasty (256–207 B.C.), communal ownership was replaced by private ownership. Abuses and difficulties multiplied, under the latter system, through the Ch'in and Han periods, by the end of which time there was much resentment on this account, and a strong demand for legislative or administrative action to check the evils of the system. Remarkable efforts were therefore made, in the period that followed the Han, to deal with the problem of landownership. To go back to the common ownership system of ancient times would have implied a great social revolution. It seems unlikely that the process went very far in that direction; but in any case controls and limitations were placed on the power and conduct of big landowners.

The period was one of great confusion and disturbance. China was subject to the incursions of various barbarian tribes, and their occupation of various areas; often the 'Han race' or Chinese proper migrated in large numbers and various directions, as a result of these pressures. At other times and places they mingled with the incoming barbarians or the people in newly colonised districts. The period is one in which direct factual evidence of any kind is extraordinarily scanty; every writer has to make some working hypothesis about it, and the door is wide open to purely subjective interpretations, or even arbitrary assumptions. Some are able partly to explain the social structure of this period by first analysing the following period;

since such-and-such features are found in the T'ang, such-and-such conditions must have existed in the preceding period, to give rise to them. Any dogmatic interpretation of this period, e.g. in terms of a specific class-struggle, or any other explanation which can hardly be supported by facts, is, however, to be regarded with extreme suspicion. The diversity of forces in this period, more perhaps than any other, is so great that it is logically impossible to reduce it to the simple formula of 'class struggle'.

NOTES TO CHAPTER XII

(1) Okazaki, *General Study of China's History*, op. cit. Chapter V, note (8).
Masumura Hiroshi, 'New Study of the White and Yellow Categories', in *Toyo Shi Kenkyu*, II, 4, 1936.

(3) Miyasaki Ichisada, 'Records of Readings', in *Shirin*, XXI, 1, 1936.

(5) Okazaki: See note (1) above; and op. cit. Chapter XI, notes (5) and (10).
Shida Fudomaro, 'Date of Establishment of the Three Grades System', in *Rekishigaku Kenkyu*, III, 6, 1934; 'Village System of Northern Wei', in *Shicho*, V, 2, 1935.
Shimizu Yasuji, 'Field System of Wei', in *Shicho*, IV, 2, 1934; '. . . of Northern Wei', *Rekishigaku Kenkyu*, Special issue, 1935; also *ibid.*, IV, 2, 1935; and in *Toyo Gakuho*, XXVI, 2.

(6) Okazaki, op. cit. Chapter XI, notes (5) and (10).
Miyakawa Hisayuki, 'Destitutes in the Wei, Chin and N. and S. Dynasties', in *To-A Jimbun Gakuho*, III, 2, 1943; 'Aristocrats in the Northern Dynasties', in *Toyoshi Kenkyu*, VIII, 4, 5, 6, 1943.

(7) Utsunomiya Kiyoyoshi, 'An Age of Tales and Neologisms', in *Kyoto Toho Gakuho*, X, 2, 1939.

(8) Niida Noboru, 'Endogamy, in the 6 Dynasties and T'ang' in *Rekishigaku Kenkyu*, IX, 8, 1939.

(9) Kato, 'China and the Military', in *Shigaku Zasshi*, L, 1, 1939.

(10) Hamaguchi, 'Segregation of Soldiers and Civilians in the time of Ts'ao Ts'ao', in *Toho Gakuho*, XI, 1, 1940; 'Soldier Households in Chin and the Southern Dynasties', in *Shigaku Zasshi*, LII, 3, 1941; 'Subordinate Generals, etc., in the Chin History', in *Toho Gakuho*, XXVII, 3 (Kyoto), 1942; 'Military Households in the N. and S. Dynasties', in *Tokyo Toho Gakuho*, XII, 1, 1941.

(11) Niida Noboru, *Shina Mibunho Shi* (History of Legal Status in China), 1942; 'Fengchien in China, Feudalism in Europe', in *Toyo Bunka*, V, 1951.

(12) Norinsho (J. Ministry of Agriculture and Forestry) Research Dept.

(13) See note (1) above.
(14) Okazaki, op. cit.
Uchida Ginzo, 'Field Allotment, etc., in Medieval Japan', in *Nihon Keizai Shi Kenkyu*, 1945, is an excellent study comparing Japan.
Similarly, an older work: Nakada Kaoru, 'The Japanese Manorial System', in *Kokka Gakkai Zasshi*, xx, 1, 1908.
And, among moderns, Niida Noboru, op. cit., Chapter IX, note (15).
Tamai Zehaku, 'T'ang Period Land Problem', in *Shina Shakai Keizai Shi Kenkyu*, 1942; Shida, op. cit., Chapter IX, note (15).
(15) Miyasaki, in *To-A Keizai Kenkyu*, XIX, 4, 1935.
(16) Miyazaki Okazaki, cit. supra.
Yoshida Torao, 'Taxation under Wei, Chin and N. and S. Dynasties', in *To-A Keizai Kenkyu*, XXI, 4, 1943.
Shimizu: op. cit., note (5) above.
(18) Sogabe Shizuo, 'Field System of Chin Wu Ti', in *Bunka*, XI, 4, 1936.
(20) Moriya Katsumi, op. cit., Chapter X, note (5).
Kato Shigeru, *Shina Shakaishi Gaisetsu*, 1939.

CHAPTER XIII

NORTHERN AND SOUTHERN DYNASTIES

Modern research has come some distance towards a 'synthetic' explanation of the formation of Chinese society from the Han Dynasty onwards. An outline of its conclusions, for the period now under consideration, would be somewhat as follows (1).

The Earlier Han period (206 B.C.–A.D. 9) saw, internally, the triumph of the 'gentry' as a new ruling class, displacing the military men of the previous period. The merchant class could by this time have contributed personnel suitable for the administration; but it was not considered eligible.

The major external influence at that time was the Hsiung Nu Empire to the north of China—the same people as the Huns, whose name is a by-word in European history also. This Hsiung Nu kingdom tried to attract Chinese emigrants, of two classes especially: intellectuals or literati, who could be administrators, and peasants. The latter would strengthen the Huns, because they would establish an agricultural basis (rather, a fringe) which would ensure the food supply of the nomad armies of the Huns, and make them a strong force, in winter as well as in summer. The early Han Emperors had to hold a nice balance, as against this neighbour. Though the Huns were much influenced by Chinese ways, they held firmly for several centuries to their traditional way of life—the habits of a nomad people. During much of that time, the Chinese Emperors actually paid tribute to them. Only in the later part of the second century B.C. did the Chinese manage to quell this neighbour, by a full frontal attack, at enormous loss to themselves.

A main Chinese motive in this move would appear to have been the growing trade with Turkestan, and the great prospects of trade with other parts of Central Asia; the reports of the famous diplomatic envoy, Chang Ch'ien, had aroused an eager interest in China. The strong Hsiung Nu State threatened to monopolise all such trade, and its advantages; it is presumably for that reason, and to wipe out the ignominy of paying tribute, and to eliminate this strategic menace, that the Chinese moved against the Hun kingdom. The Chinese had to win this struggle in the end, because the Huns, even when they had the ascendancy, had no wish to complete their victory by occupying China proper. They preferred to keep to their nomadic way of life, and returned to their own areas.

Meanwhile, with stabilisation in China, fewer and fewer Chinese sought to emigrate and to enter the Hun service. The Hsiung Nu actually resorted to kidnapping-raids, as a means of getting 'technical assistance' from China.

But other peoples, in the areas surrounding China, did not have the same desire to cling to their nomadic or tribal ways of life. The Yueh tribes in the South, the Toba, Mongols and Manchus in the North, took rather the path of adoption of Chinese ways, fusion with the Middle Kingdom—and thus, gradually, of extinction of their own individuality. The search for trade was clearly an overwhelming motive for the Chinese, in this connection, and was shared by these neighbouring peoples. Where the Hsiung Nu had rivalled the Chinese in this respect, or threatened their trade routes, these other peoples were apparently inclined to collaborate; or they were necessary intermediaries, in as much as the caravan routes ran through their territories.

The impoverishment of China at the end of the Later Han (end of the second century A.D.) must largely have been due to a double drain. One constant source of direct loss was the strife against the Hsiung Nu. This was a war of cavalry, and it drained China of horses, in particular. Horses were sought from the neighbouring areas, in great numbers, over a long period of time; they were paid for with silk, the procurement of which was financed by heavy taxation in the Middle Kingdom. The other drain, less direct in character, was in the nature of the new trade with Central Asia. It consisted very largely of the import of non-essentials and luxury articles, paid for partly in gold, but mainly in silk. The Government revenue was calculated, and taxes levied, largely in silk; the adverse trade balances fundamentally affected the State budget and finances.

Meanwhile, life and politics within China had deteriorated

into a condition of chaos, with the rise of various conflicting cliques. The tyrant Wang Mang was able to seize power; his brief reign, in which he attempted a full centralisation of control over all economic and social affairs under the State, forms a mere interlude in the long history of the Han. The Han Dynasty (henceforward known as the Later Han) was restored by an able leader (Liu Hsiu), thrown up by a tide of peasant revolt.

* * *

The Hsiung Nu appear meanwhile to have recovered strength; but, fortunately for the Chinese, they suffered a run of droughts and floods. More important, perhaps, was the fact that another kingdom had arisen to dominate the Central Asian area farther east, which balanced the power of the Hsiung Nu. In the latter part of the first century A.D., the Chinese re-established themselves in the Turkestan area—largely as a result of the personal achievements of the famous Pan Ch'ao. The latter was able to maintain an 'autonomous' Chinese army in Turkestan, which lived off the country. The Central Asian trade did not show, in this period, such an adverse balance as in the previous period. There was some commercial colonisation of the Western Regions (Turkestan) by the Chinese, and the trade was increasingly in Chinese hands at both ends, in Central Asia as well as in China.

In the meantime, however, conditions within China deteriorated. At the time of the Restoration of the Later Han (A.D. 23), the basic situation seems to have been that the population had been drastically reduced by the preceding wars and troubles, and that land was therefore relatively plentiful. Some landowners rapidly expanded their holdings and their influence, especially those with Palace connections. Nevertheless, it would be wrong, in many ways, to leap to the conclusion that this meant the 'feudalistic' oppression of the people by landowners. In the first place, there was temporarily room for everyone, and the period of the Later Han was an age of prosperity for all classes; in the second place, the landowners split into innumerable cliques and struggled against each other, far from presenting any common front of 'class' struggle against the people under them. Gradually, the population rose again to the point of full land-utilisation, the clique divisions caused increasing chaos, and luxury and over-centralisation at Court weakened the whole economy.

Three powerful generals remained; one of them (Ts'ao Ts'ao), on the background of an unsuccessful peasant revolt (the 'Yellow Turbans' movement, largely under Taoist influence), was the founder of a new dynasty, the Wei (A.D. 220). Wei consisted of the northern and north-western portions of the Han Empire. It held the most populous and productive areas of China (the plains of Shensi and Honan). It maintained a considerable trade, through Turkestan, with Central Asia. In the latter area, some states were tributary to the Wei; but the expense of maintaining this relation, by military force or subsidy, outweighed the trading profit, which became even less than it had been for the Han. On its diminished resources, the Wei tried to maintain Centralisation and Metropolitanism on the same scale as the Han; its capital city, with the Court and administration, was disproportionately large and expensive. To keep the northern frontiers, it paid the Hsiung Nu and other northern tribes, in money or grants of land, for their military assistance; while it maintained large armies, to keep in check the rival Chinese states in the south and south-west. Its internal difficulties rapidly increased, as it could not keep its own generals in check, and many of these became rich, powerful and independent.

* * *

The Shu-Han kingdom took over the Han domains in Western China. It was not large, populous or strong enough to defeat the Wei. On the other hand, it included the large granary area of Szechuan, and it could only be attacked on two small sectors of its eastern frontiers; elsewhere it was protected by wild or mountainous country. It maintained a considerable (and profitable) trade to the west and south-west, with Tibet, and even India.

The third state, of the Three Kingdoms, was Wu, occupying the Nanking area and the lower Yangtze valley. This territory was largely mountainous, or marshy, and was inhabited by barbarian tribes, some cultivating rice, others living mainly by hunting. At that time, this was not one of the granary areas of China. Its agricultural development depended firstly on Chinese immigrants from the north; these faced unfamiliar conditions—ricelands instead of wheat, or pig and poultry-farming instead of pastoral conditions. Secondly, the development of this area depended on well-organised, large-scale irrigation and water-control works, which could not be effected until a stronger social and political basis was created. Wu developed rapidly, however, in the sphere of trade—especially of transit trade. It received metals, timber, etc., from the south, and an increasing range of imports even from India and the Near East, which it passed on to North China.

On the whole, the Three Kingdoms were fairly equally balanced, strategically and materially; no one of them could make much inroad on the others, and none could reunite China. Their subsidiary and external relations are of the highest interest. Wu and Wei had intricate relations with Japan, and with the Yen State which had newly arisen in Southern Manchuria. The destiny of China began to be involved, culturally, politically and economically, with regions to the east (Manchuria, Korea, Japan) as well as with continental Asia to the west. The extension of Chinese culture to Japan, begun in the Han, proceeded thereafter apace.

Shu-Han was defeated and subjugated by Wei in 263, but almost immediately afterwards drastic changes occurred in Wei itself, which led to a breakdown of both the external and the internal equilibrium of China. Few subjects of historical study are more important today than the task of distinguishing the relative importance, in this process, of the 'internal' (Chinese) and 'external' (environmental or Asian) factors. Turkestan was still loosely attached to Wei. The Hsiung Nu were weak, though they were beginning to form a new unit (the Juan-Juan) in association with the Mongols, which later became powerful. Wei itself contained nearly a score of northern tribal groups; these were only beginning to be restive. The only immediate pressure came from the Hsien Pi tribes in eastern Mongolia. What occurred was a change of dynasty in Wei; the powerful Ssu-Ma family seized the throne, and became the Western Chin Dynasty (265–317).

The new dynasty overthrew the remaining component of the Three Kingdoms, Wu, in 280. But these efforts weakened it still further; princes and generals increased their local power, at the expense of the central. There was hardly any money or metal in the country; it had all been made into arms. The new dynasty, having quelled all the surrounding states, hastened to declare demobilisation and disarmament. This measure would at one stroke have restored central power, the coinage, agricultural production and the tax revenue. But it failed in all these respects, because the demobilised men were out of control; they deserted in large numbers, or emigrated beyond the northern frontiers, and failed to give up their arms, which largely went also to the 'outside' northern tribes.

The latter gained strength as rapidly as the Western Chin declined. Chinese emigration northward and north-westward evidently increased, providing the tribes there with further arms, and (as the Chinese settled on the land) with an increased food-supply. The history of the various tribes and groupings is complicated. The first event of outstanding importance was that the Hsiung Nu—in this case the group of nineteen Hunnish or Turki tribes who had long been on a semi-settled basis within the Wei and Western Chin frontiers—constituted themselves a Chinese dynasty, called the Former Chao, in succession to the Western Chin (A.D. 304). Thus they signalised a complete break with their nomadic and pastoral origins, claiming the cultural heritage of China, proposing to rule over the agrarian Chinese, even claiming legitimacy of descent from the Han royal family.

These claims were, however, in opposition to the Chinese regimes in the South, which were (from A.D. 317 to 419) to some extent consolidated under the 'Eastern Chin Dynasty'. The division between North and South was intensified. The Former Chao in the North was succeeded by the Later Chao (329–52), which invaded regions far to the south, but as a policy of raiding, rather than of settlement. Part of North-west China seceded, as the 'Former Liang Dynasty', keeping and developing the Turkestan trade. The Yen State in Manchuria, the Mongol groups, the Tibetan groups, all had different economic and social bases; their fortunes rose and fell, their relative significance changed in every decade. The Toba State (385–550) became the 'great power' in the northern area.

The progress of the Toba depended largely on their encouragement of Chinese immigration, which gave them a settled agricultural basis, and provided good administrators. It was economic geography and military necessity which forced them also to move their capital southwards, and to rely more on the southern (agrarian) portion of their domains than on the northern (pastoral) areas. But this development split the tribal leaders and the people into two groups, with different outlooks and different economic interests. The Toba Empire, in its turn, disintegrated. But it was a Toba aristocrat of Chinese origin who was able to seize power and establish the Sui Dynasty (581), at last reuniting China.

* * *

The whole process in the North is one of a shifting equilibrium between the nomadic peoples and cultures and the Chinese, and their eventual union through adaptation to each others' ways and requirements. In the South an essentially similar process occurred, in different circumstances and a different environment. Economic factors favoured the North, which controlled the main trade routes and held the main granaries. The story of secession and disintegration in the South is hardly less complicated than that of the North. At last the combination of circumstances occurred which enabled the Sui to reunite the whole country; political and military weakness in the South coincided with the rise, farther north, of a state (Sui) which had a political and economic interest in occupying and using the neighbouring areas, rather than in destroying them for the sake of plunder, or for its own safety.

The spread of Buddhism is an important feature of this whole period, in close connection with economic history; travel and trade were concomitants of pilgrimage, and of the procurement abroad of scriptures and images. Mercantile centres and monasteries were often found together.

The above features all contributed to the characterisation of the reunited China which emerged during the Sui Dynasty. The consolidation of the latter occupied a further forty years (580–618), and cleared the way for the next Great Empire, the T'ang. The last three chapters have dwelt at some length on this period, the formative significance of which seems very great. For it is in this period that many of the basic characteristics of China first emerge in their 'modern' forms.

NOTE TO CHAPTER XIII

(1) This period is too complicated for detailed references to be given. The present chapter attempts to summarise the conclusions in a very wide field of research. There are few good general works on this period. Chapter VII of Eberhard's recent *History of China* gives a very useful summary.

CHAPTER XIV

BASIC PROBLEMS OF T'ANG SOCIETY

The development of the T'ang Empire is immediately comparable to that of the Han, in its broadest outlines. The frontiers and alliances of the Chinese expanded similarly, into Central Asia; trade developed to the south-eastward also. Internally there was for the most part great prosperity; and a great flowering of culture makes the age immortal.

This, then, was the second of the Great Empires, another expansionist period of China's economy and life. As in the case of the preceding age of the Han, the China of that time can only be understood if it is studied in two aspects: from the internal point of view, of the nature and real basis of the specifically Chinese type of society, and from the external point of view, which considers the relationship of that society to those parts of Asia of which it was the centre.

As in the case of the Han, this is a period which is extensively and richly documented. The Japanese are vitally interested in this period, since much of their own cultural, governmental, social and other heritage derives from the T'ang in particular. Hence some of the best Japanese work relates to this period. A standard Japanese authority on the T'ang era (and also the Sung) was Tamai Korehiro. The fruits of his work are largely contained in one major work, his *Researches* (1). His standing as an authority on the T'ang has been compared with that of Okazaki on the preceding period. Much of the work of the late Dr. Kato Shigeru on this period has, however, yet to be published; when it appears, it may take the first place, in the opinion of Japanese scholars.

A similar position is held in China by Chu Ch'ingyuan, a well-known contributor to the 'Shih Huo', with his sequence of three works on the *Economic History*, *Financial History* and *State Industries* of T'ang (2). To the Japanese translation of these, the translators have appended an excellent bibliography. Another well-known Chinese work, part of which was published by the Peking University Institute of Economic History, embodied an even more ambitious plan. Under the editorship of T'ao Hsi-sheng, all the available data were to be collected (relating to the T'ang period) in eight volumes or sections. The titles given for the latter are in themselves indicative of what should be the main headings of study, from the point of view of the 'internal' analysis of the T'ang structure. They are: land problems, the temples (Buddhism) and economic life, transport and communications, agrarian legislation, urbanisation, commerce, industry and currency. Only the first three have been published (3).

The period has been covered by Japanese scholars from points of view varying from colourful romanticism (4) to formal studies in jurisprudence (5). The general or traditional inclination in Japan was to consider the key question of the T'ang period to be that of the nature and composition of the ruling class. Naito Torajiro (6) describes the period from the Six Dynasties to the middle of T'ang as an age of 'aristocracy'. Utsunomiya Kiyoyoshi agreed with him, on the basis especially of his study of genealogies and ancestral records concerning the period up to the reign of the Emperor Hsuan Tsung (A.D. 713–56) (7).

The T'ang aristocracy was not, however, the same as the aristocracy of the preceding period. Another Japanese historian, Nunome Chofu, studying the ancestry of the Chief Ministers of early T'ang times (8), showed that the nobility did not take much part in politics or public life, in which the prominent positions were taken by members of the military and civil service families, throughout the earlier part of the T'ang period. Moreover, these were largely people who were 'barbarians' in their remoter origins, coming from the Northern Dynasties. There is much evidence that, in the early T'ang times, 'blue blood' received no great respect for its own sake, though the aristocracy remained wealthy. Many proud families were ruined in the troubled times of An Lu-shan and Shih Ssu-ming. Their place was taken by a new class of 'gentry'; for, from the reign of the usurping Empress Wu (684–710) especially, there appears to have been increasingly free promotion of officials of lower class origin. The open Examination System for entry to the civil service had been established previously by the Sui.

Other scholars think these generalisations may be too sweeping; they stress further the difference between North and South. In the North, feudal and tribal conditions prevailed, tending to favour autocratic government; whereas in the South the Chinese gentry class, with the traditions of scholar-administratorship, still persisted (9). A third school might consider that even this involves too much generalisation. There certainly was not one uniform pattern in the North, and another in the South; there was a wide range of local differences in each (10).

Generally speaking, it appears that in any case both the 'tribal' Northern and 'aristocratic' Southern systems had already broken down before the Sui, perhaps long enough before to have become merely 'names and forms', with little practical content, by the time of the T'ang. The institution of free recruitment to the Government service, through Public Examinations open to all talented individuals, came by the Sui period to be the only practical alternative. How else could a 'class' or 'cadre' of government personnel be found at that time?

Presumably the Open Examination system allowed at first for considerable compromise with the various 'Northern' and 'Southern' conceptions. The 'Nine Grades' system, which gave much scope for the power politics of cliques or clans, persisted for a long time in the South, but it finally gave way to the new system.

All these considerations may seem to belong to the sphere of political or administrative history, rather than economic history proper. The economic development was, however, to a large extent conditioned by the nature of the State apparatus; the main sources of social and economic advantage, through most of China's history, have been the spoils of office. On the political and administrative issues depended, in any case, the questions of what was the 'ruling class' and what were its 'class interests'. These criteria would appear to be far more cogent than those of economic motives, from the point of view of sociological analysis.

The agrarian problem, for example, was posed ostensibly and primarily in administrative terms. The 'Field Equalisation

System' and the 'Three Grades' Local Government System, inherited from the preceding period, were still formally the basis for the solution of the land utilisation problem, and for the regulation of the communal life of the villages, respectively. Similarly 'legalistic' regulation-systems were introduced for transport and for civil (group) mobilisation procedures (i.e. census, registration, tax and labour levies) (11).

The records from the Tun Huang excavations provided a mass of information on these topics, leading to a number of useful studies. The field of analysis is extremely complicated. The broad conclusion would seem to be that the 'Field Equalisation System'—in the sense of an allotment of land by rotation—continued to be the basic principle of policy until about the middle of the T'ang Dynasty. The Chinese historians attach a great importance to it. The conception is idealised, in the same way as the 'well-field' system was idealised by Mencius and his successors (12).

From the middle of the T'ang onwards, the dominant form of agrarian organisation became rather the large estate. These large holdings are often described as a 'manorial system'; but the implied analogy with the manor as it existed in European (or for that matter, Japanese) feudalism, which seems to be automatically assumed, is a confusion of thought and terminology, which has created intellectual havoc (13).

This is by no means to say that 'land equalisation' or the growth of large estates are not very important features of the T'ang period. To leap to such a conclusion would be to err just as seriously in the opposite direction (14). The attempt to find a true perspective has involved a great deal of research and thought, on the part of those scholars who are not content to accept a ready-made party formula.

Okazaki's opinion is that the field equalisation policy was applied concurrently with the older rule of private ownership, but that the latter generally predominated. Kanai emphasises the changes of policy from one part of the period to another; at first the concern appears to have been ('negatively') to prevent the growth of excessively large holdings, but it later developed into a positive aim of actually equalising the size of holdings.

The conclusion which emerges is that these conceptions were the main features in the formal and legal outlook, the 'ideology' on which the T'ang civilisation was based. But they were far from being the sole features; important also were the conceptions of 'regulation', census-taking and regimentation of the population, for the systematic fulfilment of social and economic functions. In the practical field, the application of these ideas to actual government and production, the same conclusion applies: 'equalisation' was important, but taxation, labour service, etc., have all to be considered. The 'equalised' and 'assigned' holdings were not the only types of land tenure, for that matter; modern research attaches increasing importance to such special categories as 'benefices' held by officials, which went either with the rank or with the particular appointment held. Further, there were various types of farmers, distinguished by their work and functions on the one hand, and by their rights and privileges on the other. Of special significance is the study of the various types of exemptions (from taxes or labour dues) which were granted to farmers and others (15).

As the study of the subject progresses, the picture is becoming ever more complicated, and the simple formula of 'class-struggle' becomes ever more inadequate or untenable. The development of the large estates, in the latter half of the T'ang period particularly, led to an increase and diversification of the tenant class. This did not mean simply or entirely an intensification of 'class struggle' between tenants and landlords, however. Both groups were mixed, and there were many gradations of relationship between them; thus the generalisation into 'contending classes' is grossly inaccurate. Moreover, the agrarian system, and the volume and importance of trade, were very greatly expanding and increasing at the time. Many 'new villages', 'newly settled areas', and some commercial towns came into existence. It is not so much a question of rival classes fighting to divide a fixed area, or a fixed output (which so easily comes to mind, if one is visualising the conditions of China at a later date), as a question of the dynamic movement of different types of people expanding over a varied terrain (16).

* * *

An important and stimulating type of research, developed only in recent years, is the study of the actual techniques of agricultural and other production in each period, from the examination of both written evidences and archaeological remains. An interesting example, for the period now under consideration, is Nishijima Sadao's essay entitled *Beyond the Stone Rollers* (17). This curious title will be explained presently. The work is subtitled, 'A Problem in the History of the Development of Agricultural Productivity in North China'. It deals with the use during the T'ang period of an agricultural implement called a roller-stone, which is taken to indicate a change in the staple crop of North China, in that period, from millet to wheat. The thesis refers also to the growing intensification of cultivation, largely due to the development of towns and cities; and to the increase of large estates, seen from the technical point of view as connected with the introduction of wheat as the basic crop. The growing of wheat, on larger areas, is shown to have changed all ideas of crop rotation. The history of 'field equalisation' in the period is then treated in terms of a governmental attempt to preserve the production of rice, which was being displaced in various localities by wheat. Later, when this attempt had been finally unsuccessful, various tax, levy and labour service measures were imposed, the Government now accepting the dominance of wheat, the use of stone rollers, new ideas of irrigation, and the conversion of ricefields into dry fields.

This very original work contributes significantly to our understanding of the period. It represents a technique of investigation and deduction which is proving very fruitful in this field, and is increasingly being utilised, in Japan especially. A comparison may be made with the studies, in European Economic History, which analysed the evolution of milling, from the point of view of its technical development and social effects (18).

The attention of students of this period has very largely been concentrated on its agrarian aspects, with the question of land utilisation always in the foreground. Considerable work has been done on such other aspects as public finance, currency, etc. But these and other subjects require to have much further work done upon them, and it seems fair to say that they have not yet led to the formulation of any very suggestive conclusions of an overall nature.

The above may serve to give an impression of the state of work, from the point of view of investigation of the 'internal' character of the T'ang period. In the following chapter, an overall description of the T'ang economy will be attempted, from the 'external' point of view of its relations with the Asian environment outside.

NOTES TO CHAPTER XIV

(1) Tamai, *Shina Shakai Keizai Kenkyu*, 1937.
(2) Japanese translation, Rokubana and Okamoto, 1941.
(3) With (2) above. Japanese translation, Nakajima, 1934.
(4) Ishida Mikinosuke, *Choan no Haru*, cit. supra, *Toshi Sojo*, 1948.
(5) Niida Noboru, *To-So Hoken Bunsho so Kenkyu*, 1937; *To Rei Shu-I*, 1933.
(6) Naito, *Gaikatsu-teki To-So Jidai Kan*; *Chukoku Jokoshi*, 1943; *Chukoku Kindaishi*, 1947.
(7) Utsunomiya, 'Observations on the Tang Aristocracy', in *Shirin*, XIX, 3, 1934.
(8) Nunome, 'Aristocrats of Early Tang', in *Toyoshi Kenkyu*, X, 3, 1945.
(9) Tamai, op. cit. supra. Niida, 'Titles and appointments in the Tang period', in *Toho Gakuho*, Tokyo, X, 1, 1938.
Miyazaki, 'Wang An-shih's Policy', in *Essays for Dr. Kuwahara's 60th Birthday*, 1931.
(10) Hamaguchi Shigekuni, 'Land Taxation in Tang', *Toyo Gakuho*, XX, 1, 1936; 'Rice Collection and Taxation under Tang Hsuan Ti', in *Shigaku Zasshi*, XLV, 2, 1934.
(11) Miyazaki, 'Optional Notes', cit. supra. Sogabe Shizuo, 'Study of Group Regimentation', in *Toyoshi Kenkyu*, IX, 3, 1920.
(12) Ou-Yang Hsiu, 1936.
Suzuki Toshi, 'Field Equalisation Law and Tang Decrees', in *To-A*, VII, 4, 1933; 'Relation between Field-equalisation, tax and Corvée in the Tang Period', in *To-A*, VIII, 4, 1934; 'Household Registration in the Tang Period', in *Shigaku Zasshi*, XLVII, 7, 1936.
Kanai Shichu, 'Treatise on Tang Field Equalisation', in *Bunka*, X, 5, 1943.
(13) Wada Kiyoshi, 'On the National Policy of China', in *Orientalica*, I, 1948. Tamai, *Todai Dochi Mondai Kanken*, 1944.
(14) Nawa Toshisada, 'Households and Population in the T'ienpao Era', in *Rekishi to Chiri*, XXXIII, 1–4, 1934.

Niida, *To Rei Shu-I*, 1933. Naito, op. cit. supra, note (6) above. Okazaki, 'On the Tang Field Equalisation Law', in *Shinagaku*, II, 1934. Kanai, op. cit., note (12) above.

(15) Niida, 'Systems of Private Landownership in Ancient China and Japan', in *Kokka Gakkai Zasshi*, XLIII, 12, and XLIV, 7, 8, 1942; and op. cit. note (5) above. Osaki Seiji, 'Post Fields in the Tang Capital', in *Shicho*, XII, 3, 4, 1943. Hamaguchi, 'Military and Labour Service in Tang', in *Toyo Gakuho*, XX, 4, and XXI, 1, 1936. Sogabe Shizuo, 'Taxation of Persons under Tang', in *Shirin*, XXIX, 1, 1944; 'Labour Service in the Jih-Tang Decrees', in *Shigaku Zasshi*, LV, 8, 1944; 'District Garrisons, etc.', in *Bunka*, I, 10, 1934; 'On Filial Piety, etc.', in *Shigaku Zasshi*, VI, 7, 1937. Niida, 'System of Labour Service in the Tang Decrees', in *Shigaku Zasshi*, VI, 3, 1937.

(16) Okada Takumi, 'Development of the Manor under Tang', in *Keisai Shi Kenkyu*, XIV, 6, 1936. Nakada, 'The Japanese Manor', in *Kokka Gakkai Zasshi*, XX, 10, 1936. Kato Shigeru, 'Nature and Origin of the Tang Manor', in *Toyo Gakuho*, VII, 3, 1933; *On Land Utilisation, etc.*, in *ibid.*, X, 2, 1936; 'Organisation of Tang and Sung Manors', in *Essays for Dr. Kano's 60th Birthday*, 1928. Hamaguchi, 'Land Tax of Tang', in *Toyo Gakuho*, XX, 1, 1936. Suzuki Toshi, 'The Household Taxes and the Green Shoot scheme', in *Essays for Dr. Ikegammi's 60th Birthday*, 1940. Kanai Shichu, 'Summer and Autumn Taxes', *ibid.* Chu Ching-yuen, 'Household Tax of Tang', in *Shih Huo*, I, 8, 1935. Yoshida Torao, 'Double Taxation under the Tang', in *To-A Keizai Kenkyu*, XXIV, 2, 1940; 'Critique of the Tax System of Tang', in *Shigaku Zasshi*, LI, 7, 1940; 'Taxation after An Lu-shan and Shih Ssu-ming', in *Bunka*, XI, 2, 1944. Kobayashi Koshiro, 'Double Tax System of Tang', in *Shakai Keizai Shigaku*, III, 6, 1932.

(17) In *Rekishi Gaku Kenkyu*, CXXV, 1946.

(18) Takigawa Masajiro, 'A Study of Stone Rollers', in *Shakai Kagaku*, I, 7, 1946. Hatano Yoshihiro, 'Progress in understanding Chinese History', in *Rekishigaku Kenkyu*, CXXXIX, 1949.

CHAPTER XV

THE GREAT T'ANG EMPIRE

In the last chapter, the problems of landownership and agriculture were given special emphasis. It is chiefly the Japanese writers who place well in the foreground this aspect of the 'internal' problems of the period. They render a good service in doing so. The fundamental instability of this otherwise brilliant and flourishing epoch will never be fully understood, until the deep background of its rural crisis has been appreciated. This is another major field of study in this subject, of special importance; though the variety of trends and forms, and the confusion of their effects, is so great that we may perhaps never solve the riddles of the time.

It may be sufficient to say of the internal nature of the T'ang society, on the planes particularly of administration and agriculture, that it represented a confused situation, numerous and conflicting features and tendencies inherited from the preceding epoch of division and strife, which was never resolved into a generalised and co-ordinated society. Social stability and solidity appear distinctly less in rural matters, at least, than they were in—for example—the Han. Yet the T'ang was, much more than the Han—or for that matter almost any other age of China—an era of great intellectual and practical stimulation, of progress and 'dynamism', as Japanese writers have called it. Following the method used in the foregoing chapters, we may now see how the 'external' approach has been able to clarify and rationalise our understanding of this period.

First, it is necessary to consider that there was initially a time of consolidation. The fluid and fragmented state of what we may call, borrowing a convenient phrase from recent United States procedures, 'the general area of China', was firmly and thoroughly consolidated. At least in its overall government: the enclosing framework at least was stoutly constructed, through the period of the Sui and the early T'ang, even though it was apparently not possible to set in order everything that this framework enclosed, or to solve some of the great problems that remained within.

The founder of the Sui Dynasty, Wen Ti, was no theorist, but a practical soldier. North and South must be brought under a unified command. Manpower and supplies were most unequally distributed in the various parts of the country, with (in a purely relative sense) over-population in the North, but food and materials more plentifully produced in other parts of the country. This situation had to be corrected, but as economically as possible, since no reserves or resources were available. Such must have been his appreciation of the situation.

He proceeded to move the capital to Loyang, nearer to the main 'granary' area. He unified and improved the canal system, on a grand scale. This was an entirely new aspect of 'water control policy', and of the influence of waterways on history. A number of small canals had for a long time existed. Only from the time of the Sui would canals appear to have been of major importance as a means of transport, and especially for the supply of the capital city. The Sui were able to use canal boats of up to 800 tons capacity.

This investment in the canals could not, however, yield full returns in the short period of the Sui (580–618); it was the T'ang that got the benefit later. In any case, the Sui spent their efforts, in all other directions, in ventures far less profitable than the canals. Pending the consolidation of China proper, they were obliged to fight the Turks and Koreans on the frontiers, to intrigue against them with other tribes, or to buy them off with bribes. The second Sui Emperor appears, in contrast to his father, to have been inefficient and wasteful. He lost the support of the gentry class, and his Empire collapsed.

A military commander, Li Shih-min, seized power and established the T'ang Dynasty (618–906). The Land Equalisation policy began to be applied in the early years of the dynasty. There was a complete reform of the administration in 624. This gave power over large areas to Provincial Governors, but it was a great improvement in efficiency. A striking feature was the introduction of specialised departments, rather like the Ministries of Occidental countries some centuries later, with specific charge of all matters in their respective technical fields of competence. Late in the T'ang period, an Economic Affairs Department was added, well staffed by experts: economic and financial matters were at last recognised as a reputable sphere of competence for the scholar-administrator. The internal trade and business of the country greatly increased: the movement of 800-ton cargoes by canal, in contrast to the thin flow of goods in earlier periods, is vivid evidence.

The new system facilitated a great upswing of economic activity. Budgets, tax collections, outputs, currency in circulation, and many other matters came to be measured in millions; China's economy began to assume really large national proportions. As is well known, this was also a great age of sea travel and maritime trade, and there were very substantial contacts, especially with the Arabs, but also with many other peoples.

During the seventh century, relations with Turkestan were a main preoccupation of the T'ang. The prolonged struggle with the Turks ended, after great fluctuations, in a Chinese victory over the Turkestan people. The powerful Turkish Empire remained, however, a formidable menace, holding all the area from Central Asia to the Mediterranean. The Turkestan trade was a major motive of the T'ang Chinese, in their westward thrust, just as it had been for the Chinese of the Han period some nine centuries earlier. Just as in the Han period, it turned out to be expensive, to the extent of becoming ultimately a net drain on China; and in the same ways as it had been in the Han period: namely, the expense of garrisoning the westernmost frontier and maintaining the long lines of communication, the scattering of resources, the fundamentally adverse terms of trade, and the development of a traffic in luxury goods at the expense of more urgent essentials.

T'ai Tsung's reign (627–49) marks the peak of the T'ang power. Besides Turkestan, the South was consolidated, Nam Yueh (the Viet Nam of our own day) was occupied, and the Koreans were defeated. The basis of the T'ang was stronger than that of the Han, in this period, in one important respect particularly: there was not the over-centralisation that had prevailed in the Han period. All the activities mentioned above, and the whole of the cultural developments of the T'ang period, were not over-centralised in the metropolis; the other major towns, and various parts of the country, participated richly and fully.

One school of thought traces a considerable development of 'capitalism' in this period. Certainly the monetary system, and money valuations, together with a great (and, for the first time, really widespread) development of mercantile activities, featuring the emergence of a larger and more developed merchant-class, are strong features of the period. Curiously enough—as it may seem to the Western reader—the spread of Buddhism contributed markedly to this sort of development. As noted above in discussing the initial spread of Buddhism in the Han era, this religion particularly promoted travel, and the obtaining of books, etc., from lands to the west. Now, in the T'ang era, the temples and other Buddhist foundations came to be richly endowed with lands and funds. They accumulated large quantities of the metals used for coinage. The currency history of the period is a long and complicated record of monetary vicissitudes, with coinage needs competing always with the non-monetary demand for the metals—bronze bells, images, golden ornaments, etc.—from the Buddhist institutions. Temples, monasteries, etc., became great landowners; they also held large sums in currency and in uncoined metal, and had large current incomes. Thus they were to a large extent the source of ready capital and funds or credit, in this development of 'early capitalism' in China.

In the ninth century, however, the T'ang Government turned on the Buddhist institutions, 'liquidated' Buddhism as an organised religion, and expropriated it thoroughly. The explanation of this development may furnish an excellent illustration of the interconnection between 'external' and 'internal' factors in Chinese history. During the eighth century, the external situation had greatly deteriorated. The Tibetans pressed very heavily on China. Following the principle, which had by then been thoroughly established, of 'setting the far-away barbarian against the near-by barbarian', the T'ang secured the aid of the Uighurs, a people who had rebelled against the Turks in the seventh century. The Uighurs secured in return a privileged position in trade and financial activities in the T'ang territory. They developed a considerable role as capitalists, middlemen, etc., and in this they were largely associated with the Buddhist institutions, which were (as explained above) the 'banking and financial system' of the time. Buddhism, having such a strong grip on the economic as well as the 'ideological' life of the Empire, would probably have come in for suppression by the Government in any case. But this association with foreign groups—there were others, as well as the Uighurs—was an additional reason.

Moreover, the Government was in dire need of funds and material; the suppression of Buddhism was not motivated by objections to that religion in particular, so much as by sheer need to fill the empty coffers. If there had been any other equally important source to supply the needs of the capital levy, it would have been 'raided' also by the authorities, whatever its social, political or spiritual nature. Taoism was exempted from this expropriation; however, many of the gentry class adhered to this cult, usually in addition to their profession of Confucianism. But all foreigners were expropriated.

The scholar-gentry developed in this period many of the attributes of a 'ruling class'. The development of the art of administration, and the improvements in its practice, greatly clarified the nature of the functions of these people. They lost their aloofness, their general position of vague 'superiority', and became functionaries in close and practical touch with worldly affairs and materialistic activities. They even became, in many cases, specialists and practitioners in spheres hitherto not considered appropriate even to the notice of a scholar—such as hydraulic engineering or financial policy, for example. The infusion of new elements into the gentry-class (or grade) may have contributed to this evolution. The survivors of the old type of scholar-gentry were joined, in the T'ang period, by a new type of people, from those families or clans who had supported the T'ang and helped Li Shih-min's faction in the establishment of the dynasty. These were often good military commanders, local political leaders, or men with a practical bent of mind.

While money-capital or circulating capital was accumulating in the hands of the temples and of foreign immigrants particularly, the fundamental form of 'capital', the real basis of both rank and wealth, and the ultimate form of fixed capital and investment was, however, still—the land. This has remained the case, in China, right up to modern times. It was landownership that interested the T'ang gentry, from the material point of view, and it was as landowners that they developed socially and politically.

They may have tended to use Buddhism, as well as Confucianism, as a doctrine well adapted to keeping the lower classes in their places; Buddhism taught fatalism, or acceptance of one's position in this world, the vanity of human wishes, and the futility or meaninglessness of struggle. But they could not carry this very far, if they wanted the people to work hard in their service. They seem rather to have promoted new and progressive forms of farm tenancy, especially those most likely to give a personal incentive to the peasant.

Another important objection to the 'economic class' interpretation of this period is that the leading element in the T'ang Government was generally the military one. It is well known that the T'ang is almost the only age in which the Chinese have held soldiers in real honour. Ever since the Han, there had been two 'wings' of government and administration—a civil and a military. This continued to be essentially the case, down to the end of the Manchu Dynasty. In the T'ang period, the military side predominated, almost throughout. Within the gentry class, there were many and constant divisions and conflicts of interest. These were most vividly shown in the period at the end of the seventh century when the Empress Wu seized the throne, and the gentry were divided, to the point of civil war, between support and opposition to her.

The Empress Wu greatly assisted the progress of Buddhism, making it practically a State cult. For various reasons, the decline of the T'ang may be reckoned to date from her Regency and reign (683–705). The later stages of this decline are associated with two different sets of factors: the over-extension of the Empire, which was basically unprofitable, and the increasing strife between clan-groups and military governors. Peasant revolts shook the fabric of the Empire; finally, another military leader took power, and established the first of the Five Dynasties.

In broad outline, the T'ang era may be said to repeat the cycle and the pattern observed under the Han Dynasty, some seven centuries earlier. But obviously it represented a much more advanced stage of evolution, at a much 'higher technical level'. It is too much, however, to speak of this epoch as 'medieval', in any true sense of the term. The T'ang epoch is still precursory, not intermediary, to the emergence of the 'modern' form of Chinese society. The implied comparison with European economic history is particularly misleading. The T'ang period can hardly be said to show the emergence of a 'bourgeoisie', even if it be allowed that some functions of such a class were developed (by aliens especially) in China at that time. And there are many features of the period which, while they need a great deal more study and explanation, are clearly inconsistent with any analysis of the period in terms of economic determinism (1).

NOTES TO CHAPTER XV

(1) The above is a synoptic view, attempting to interpret very widely the consensus of Occidental opinions on the period at the present time. The latter are expressed in general histories of China, rather than in particular works on this period. Apart from writings mentioned in other chapters, the following may be referred to here:

Academia Sinica, Institute of Philological and Historical Studies, 'Materials on the Economic History of China: Volume on T'ang', 1938.

Aoyama Sadao, 'Study on the Pien Canal', in *Toho Gakuho*, I, 49, 1931.

Balazs, Stefan, 'Beiträge zur Wirtschaftsgeschichte der T'ang-zeit', *Mitteilungen des Seminars für orientalische Sprachen*, Berlin, XXXIV, I, 92, 1931; XXXV, I, 73, 1932; XXXVI, I, 62, 1933.

Chao Wen-jui, 'Main points in the Trade of the T'ang period', in *Tsing Hua Journal*, III, 951, 1926.

Ch'en Chun-ju, 'The Grand Canal', in *Tribute of Yu*, VI, 27, 1936.

Cheng Te-K'un, 'Excavation of T'ang Dynasty tombs', in *Harvard Journal of Asiatic Studies*, IV, I, 1939.

Chu Ch'ing Yuan, 'House Tax of T'ang', in *Shih Huo*, I, 8, 1935; *Financial History of T'ang*, 1938 (Japanese translation by Nakajima, 1944); and *Economic History of the T'ang Period*, 1936 (Japanese translation by Rokubana and Okamoto, 1942).

Des Rotours, R., *Le Traité des Examens*, Bibliothèque de l'Institut des Hautes Etudes, Paris, 1932.

Fu An-hua, 'Cross-section of Social life in the T'ang Period', in *Wen Hua Chien She Yueh K'an*, III, November 1936.

Kato Shigeru, *Precious Metals in T'ang and Sung periods*, Tokyo, 1932.

Kobayashi Koshiro, 'Two Tax Systems of T'ang', in *Shakai Keizai Shigaku*, III, 6, 1934.

Li Ts'ai-chang, Study of the Trade of the T'ang Dynasty', in *Shih-ta Yueh-k'an*, II, June 1936.

CHAPTER XVI

THE FIVE DYNASTIES AND THE RISE OF SUNG (900–1200)

In respect of the Economic History of China during the whole period from the end of the T'ang (A.D. 906) right up to modern times, comparatively little exists in the way of published work. Books or articles to which students may be referred, for the detailed or analytical study of the subject, are far less numerous for this later period than for the preceding periods. There are some special and general studies—both those which take a wide sweep of time, and discuss the general trends or principles of this large expanse of historical development, and those which are concerned with a close examination of certain special questions and particular periods. But the bibliography (in respect of specialised and definitive economic treatises, at least, as distinct from general historical accounts) will be found to be much more restricted, relative to the great length and complexity of the post-T'ang period, than that relating to more ancient times.

It will therefore only be possible, in the following pages, to plead for a very great extension of academic interest and research effort in this field; to indicate the broad questions which arise in it; and to give, in less detail than the foregoing, an outline of the general course of economic development in China over the last ten centuries.

The period immediately following the T'ang is a most significant one, from the point of view especially of the emergence of new economic factors in the internal situation. This period is termed the 'Five Dynasties' (A.D. 906–60). It represented another division of China into a number of states, with temporary and changing dynasties—but again with a main line of difference between North and South. In some at least of the states and reigns, the features of 'capitalism', the growth of mercantile wealth and activity, and other signs or portents of development towards the more modern type of society, are very marked. It is hard to understand why the spokesmen of economic determinism mostly distinguish the T'ang period as the end of the Middle Ages, the breakdown of the older society and the emergence of the forces which (in their theory) dominate and characterise the newer order. These considerations would apply much more clearly to the Five Dynasties period. More satisfactory are those determinists who suggest rather the interpretation that certain features 'took shape' during the T'ang period, but emerged into institutional reality only in the tenth century or later.

The 'Five Dynasties' refers to the successive rulers of the northern part of the country, accounted the legitimate successors of the T'ang: namely, the dynasties of the Liang (906–23), Later T'ang (923–36), Later Chin (936–46), Later Han (947–50) and Later Chou (954–8). Among these, and between them and the surrounding northern peoples, there was constant movement and conflict; and there was in the middle of the period the intrusion of one distinctive 'dynasty of conquest' from the north, the Liao or Khitan Empire (1). The situation in the southern part of the country was even more fluid and confused; this region was divided into a number of states, the domains of rulers who may be described as provincial governors or warlords who had set up separate kingdoms.

A study of the economic differences between these districts and regimes sheds a great deal of light on the evolution of China during that period. The strongest states were two of the kingdoms in the south, which were in the nature of 'key economic areas', enjoying greater peace and prosperity than other parts of the country.

One of these was Shu, whose territory covered roughly that of the modern province of Szechuan. This was a major rice-producing area, and also a main producer of tea and salt. The drinking of tea had spread in the north-west since the third century; by the T'ang period, it was a general habit in China, so that a large trade in tea had developed, in which the people of Shu took a large part.

The other southern state which enjoyed a comparable security and prosperity was the Wu-Yueh, holding the area of the present Chekiang province. Its seaboard had figured as the gateway for trade and contacts to the north and east—with north-eastern China, Korea and Japan. Its people were active also in overland trade in tea and many other commodities. The delta of the lower Yangtse was fertile; but, broadly speaking, the main producing centre for the most important and profitable staples of trade appears to have been Shu, while the people of Wu-Yueh (and to a lesser extent those of Wu, the state lying between Shu and Wu-Yueh) also became great traders. They were well placed to develop both the trade in tea and salt, which was mainly in a west–east direction, and those other exchanges which were mainly in a north–south direction, in which northern products (such as furs) were exchanged for those of the south (such as timber). The states to the south of Shu and Wu-Yueh—Ch'u, Min and the Southern Han—were less developed and less secure.

The emergence in this way of a marked regional specialisation and division of labour within the area of China proper, greater than had previously been known, is a feature of outstanding interest. It points the moral that historically, in China as in other countries, the greatest economic progress—and progress in all other social matters, in so far as they depend on the material basis of life—is associated with the development of local initiatives, the diversification of products and activities in different regions, and the maximisation of trade and exchanges between them. Wherever and whenever a 'monolithic' system has been imposed, with centralised control and the cultivation or imposition of economic and social uniformity in all the districts, the conditions have been relatively static, and such states or periods have not been regarded by posterity as having been among the most 'dynamic', from the point of view of progress and development, or among those of greatest achievement, from the point of view of the people at large.

The Sui and T'ang system, in its prime, was such a system of metropolitanism and central control. A one-way stream of tribute flowed to the capital; and, significantly, the goods taken as tribute from any one area of the country were very largely of the same kinds as those taken in any other area. During the T'ang period, this system broke down. One of the most important subjects for research is the extent to which it broke down, and why and how it did so. As noted in the preceding chapter, this question has been studied chiefly from the point of view of the external relations: the tribute-wealth was drained away in military operations, and in a basically unprofitable export trade with a neighbouring country. (The analogy with present-day conditions is only too painfully clear.) But the question needs to be extensively studied also from the point of view of internal factors—the influences within the country which contributed to a breakdown of the system.

The above is necessarily a broad generalisation, and the contrast between the periods of the T'ang and the Five Dynasties must not be overdrawn. The trade development in the latter period was heavily subject to monopolies. The larger groups of merchants, especially in the wholesale tea trade, squeezed out the smaller dealers, and secured some general control of business credit. Further, they secured the connivance and collusion of the high officials of the governments. This was perhaps a turning-point in Chinese economic history. Hitherto, commerce had generally been 'regulated' and the merchants kept down; now there appears for the first time, not accidentally but as a characteristic, this collusion between officials and money magnates, which was thereafter to be a recurrent social and political evil.

The T'ang had attempted to make a State monopoly of the tea trade in 784, for the sake of revenue, and in order to 'regulate' this new and disturbing factor in the Chinese society. It seems to have succeeded only in maintaining a working arrangement with the wholesalers and larger dealers, for the suppression of smuggling; such, at any rate, was the situation in the succeeding period. Much the same happened in the case of salt, the other staple commodity of Shu.

The major development of the porcelain industry ('china') is another formative influence of this period. Its manufacture, which grew up in South-east China near the site of the best clay-beds, at the famous Chin Teh Chen, called for a relatively large scale of capital and organisation from the start. A nation-wide trade in chinaware quickly grew, and extended into a considerable export to Western Asia, India, the South Seas (Malaysia) and Japan. In this case also the tendency to monopolistic control is observable; but by reason of the large concentration of production, rather than in the distribution stages, or in official connivance.

This is the age also of the general spread of printing. The effects, in terms of literature, art and intellectual progress, are evident and familiar; but the economic effects of this new medicine have not been specifically studied to any great extent. Whether or not it is possible to make any assessment of that kind, this development must be appreciated as an indication of the emergence of a nation-wide (potentially, even universal) market, of all the possibilities of 'publicity' (commercial as well as political or educational), standardisation and other features which are taken for granted in the modern age.

In this period, the printing of a kind of paper money began; this was quite an established usage in the Sung period (by about A.D. 1000), but in the latter part of the T'ang, and in the Five Dynasties, this procedure was neither a regular practice, nor had it yet evolved into its modern form. The state of affairs was rather as follows. In times when there was a local dearth of copper coins (which was a fairly frequent occurrence in this period, either by reason of particular districts having a chronically adverse balance of trade, or because local governors interfered with the free flow of coins), merchants began to issue 'deposit certificates' or commodity vouchers. These soon began to circulate as a means of payment. A banking system, in the rudiment of its modern form, was thus first created. In effect, it was run by the wholesaling merchants. Soon the Government began to issue its own deposit certificates—against tax payments, deliveries of monopolised commodities, deposits of copper or coins, etc. A rudimentary conception of central banking—or, at least, State banking—thus arose. The Government certificates were sometimes printed, and these may be considered the first instances of paper currency, in so far as they were transferable.

* * *

Each of the Five Dynasties, holding the northern half of the country, was short-lived. Internal conditions were unstable for military and political reasons rather than economic ones. This is supposed to have been a period in which the Chinese 'gentry' class, of landowner-administrators, further consolidated its position by continuing to serve under various rulers—some Chinese, some northern tribesmen, some mixed. One man may play the Vicar of Bray in this way, without his character changing; but it is doubtful whether a whole class can do so without changing its composition or its characteristics. This, perhaps, is one of the special weaknesses of the 'class' interpretation of history; another respect in which it tries to 'have things both ways'. The gentry class is supposed to have adapted itself with great quickness and ingenuity to all sorts of social alignments and local circumstances; yet to have emerged unchanged, or more like its old self than ever.

Evidently, as in preceding periods, there was a very wide mingling and interchange between the classes and peoples of China and those around its borders. The process of mutual assimilation continued. Possibly it was simpler and less many-sided than in preceding periods. The main northern 'race' was at this time the Khitans, a tribal league which consolidated its own Empire all along the Manchurian and Mongolian borders. On the western, Tibetan, frontier also there was only one political-racial contender, the T'u Fan. The kingdoms in the south of China, especially Shu and Wu-Yueh, constantly 'squeezed' the northern part of China, ruled by the Five Dynasties, not only by trade pressures, but also by diplomatic and military alliances with the Turki, Khitans and T'u Fan. At the same time, however, they were trying to squeeze each other in similar ways; and the whole was a most unsteady equilibrium.

* * *

Though the new economic forces were thus more developed and more pressing in the South it was from the North that the new unification of China came. The Sung Dynasty was founded by a militarist who had the wisdom to cease the long and wasteful struggle with the northern tribes, and turn to the southward. The southern kingdoms were in any case smaller and weaker than the North; as soon as the latter came under effective leadership, it was able to annex the southern states. And the fact was that the Khitan, satisfied with their own Empire in the area of Peking and in Manchuria and Mongolia, had no urgent need or desire to extend their dominion farther south over China. Whether it was good judgment on the part of the Sung founder because he realised these facts, or just his luck, is not altogether certain; but probably the former, as clearly he was intelligent and a good organiser. He occupied the whole of South China by 980, and established a protectorate over Annam.

A significant feature of the Sung period is therefore the further development of domestic trade in South China, and a great development of foreign trade through South China ports —first with Indo-China, then overseas to all Southern and Western Asia. This trade was profitable; in contrast to the trade of the T'ang and Han periods with Central Asia, it brought in goods (still mainly luxuries, but now also some raw materials and useful things) without draining China of the precious metals, and the (not much less precious) textiles. The export of porcelain, in particular, was profitable, and that industry made great advances in the Sung period, as every connoisseur knows. Tax revenue enormously increased.

Meanwhile, the Khitan were held off by the payment of tribute, but Western accounts seem to be exaggerated, when they term this a 'Danegeld', because the amount was relatively small, and in any case much smaller than that of the maintenance of large armies and protracted campaigns, such as had previously sapped the strength of the Great Empires of China. (The moral is, once again, bitterly evident for the China of the present day—when overseas trade with the West and South would be very profitable and would serve constructive purposes, whereas the overland northern trade (or tribute?) is bleeding China, as also is the policy of building large armies, armaments and military adventures beyond the frontiers.) It is significant that one of the first measures of the Sung (963) was the abolition of the old separation between military and civil administrations, and the placing of all legislative and executive powers in the hands of civilian offices.

Generals and officers were pensioned off: the soldiers were

disbanded, many of them being settled as peasants in under-populated or newly recovered areas.

So long as the above remained the bases of policy (i.e. at least till the end of the tenth century) Sung China prospered and progressed. But in the eleventh and twelfth centuries, these original policies were gradually reversed: the military interest again became a burden on the country, the agrarian question and 'landlordism' again became acute problems, the commercial and international outlook was again replaced by anti-foreignism and a new foreign menace arose outside—the dire and ruthless military power of the Mongols, which finally spelled the doom of peaceful China.

The downfall of the Sung and the period of the Mongol occupation will be reviewed in the next chapter. Meanwhile some attention must be paid to another main feature of the 'rising' and 'prosperous' phases of the Sung era; i.e. the following. The enormous and unprecedented increase in the State revenues led to an enormous increase in State initiative, control and enterprise, to a degree quite unprecedented in China (since the time of the 'Socialist Emperor' of antiquity, Chin Shih Huang Ti) and indeed not matched in succeeding periods (until the time of the first Communist Leader, Mao Tse-tung, Shih Hung Ti).

The best known instances of 'State Socialist' policies in the Sung period are those of Wang An-shih. It is possible that these were however devised primarily as measures against the excessive predominance of wholesale traders and large entrepreneurs over retailers and shopkeepers or craftsmen, and in support of the smaller landowners against the larger, rather than as a positive conception of State Socialism, a 'new deal' or a Nationalisation theory. Moreover, the whole question of Wang An-shih's purposes and policies, and those of his opponents, is so much wrapped up in issues and motives other than the economic ones, that it cannot be discussed only on the economic plane (2).

There are, however, other instances besides those of Wang An-shih, to which more attention might be paid. Notably (at a later stage, in the Southern Sung period) there is the land reform movement of Chia Ssu-tao, which lasted for ten years, and was largely responsible for the defection of the landlords, which sealed the final doom of Sung China. Meanwhile, the State operated many 'welfare' policies, in addition to the well-known schemes of Wang An-shih—schemes for the care of aged people, the free burial of the poor, orphanages, government medicine shops, etc. The State also operated—for the sake of getting revenue—restaurants, taverns, etc. In Hangchow in 1288, there were actually more than two score of state-owned brothels, according to some interpretations of the records.

All these things were done to increase and regularise the receipt of revenue, and to maintain the conception of the State, particularly of the paternal State as the regulator of internal social differences, standing above the classes, and having the responsibility for checking the undue influence of landlords, or of any other sectional interest. Clearly the motives of economic self-interest do not suffice to give an analysis of the China of this period, nor can it be very far explained as the dominance of any one class. Landowners and merchants may however have been powerful and recalcitrant enough to have played a considerable part in pulling down the structure of Sung China. Some of them certainly went over to the Mongols, as soon as these appeared in the role of the succeeding power. But it is stretching the evidence too far to suggest either that they constituted a coherent class in themselves, or that they exerted an autonomous and decisive influence on the course of events (3).

NOTES TO CHAPTER XVI

(1) Wittfogel, *Liao*, cit. supra.
(2) Williamson, *Wang An Shih*, 2 vols., 1936.
(3) Additional bibliography:
Akizawa Shuji, *Shina Shakai Kosei*, 1939.
Ch'en Ts'an, *Chung Kuo Shang Yeh Shih*, 1925 (Japanese translation by Maruyama Shosaburo, 1943).
Chou Ku-Sheng, *Chung Kuo Cheng-jih Shih*, 1940; *Chung Kuo T'ung Shih*, 1939.
Chu Ch'ing-yuan, op. cit., Chapter XIII, note (2).
Franke, O., *Geschichte des chinesischen Reiches*, Berlin-Leipzig, 1930–7 (Japanese translation by Takayama, 1938).

Herrman, A., *Historical and Commercial Atlas of China*, Harvard, 1935.
Hozumi Fumio, *Shina Kahei Ko*, 1944 (Chinese Coinage).
Imabori Seiji, 'The T'ang Gentry', in *Rekishigaku Kenkyu*, IX, 11, and X, 2, 1939–40.
Kaino Toritaka, *Shina Tochi Kampoho Joretsu* (Introduction to Land-usages of China), 1938.
Kato Shigeru, *Shina Keizai Shi Gaisetsu*, 1944; *Shina no Shakai*, 1935; *Shina Keizai Shi no Kaitaku*, 1948; *Shina Keizai Shi*, 1927.
Lo Chung-yen, *Chung Kuo Kuo-min Ching-chi Shih*, 1937.
Lu Ssu-mien, *Chung Kuo T'ung-shih*, 1940.
Miyazaki Ichisada, *Toyoteki Sekai*, 1950 (contains a good description of the special features of the Northern Sung).
Moriya Katsumi, *Shina Shakai Keizai Shi*, 1934 (Chinese translation by Sun Huai-jen, 1936).
Niida Noboru, 'T'ang decrees', in *Shigaku Zasshi*, VI, 3, 1896.
Okazaki Fumio, 'Field System of T'ang', in *Shina-gaku*, II, 7, 1923; with Naha Toshisada, Aritaka Iwao and Kotake Fumio, *Shina Shakai Shi*, 1941.
Suzuki Toshi, 'Field Equalisation of T'ang', in *To-A*, VIII, 4, 1934.
Sakharoff: Japanese translation of this Russian Marxist author's work (original unknown to present writer) by Hayakawa Jiro, 1934, is very popular in Japan.
Sogabe Shizuo and Hozumi Fumio, *Shina Keizai Shi*, 1941.
T'ao Hsi-sheng, 'Loans and usury laws of T'ang' (*She-hui K'o-hsueh*, II, 1936); 'Market regulations of T'ang' in *Shih Huo*, IV, 1936; 'Water regulations of T'ang', *ibid.*
Tseng Yang-feng, *Chung Kuo Yen Cheng Shih* (History of Salt Administration in China), 1936 (Japanese translation by Yoshimura, 1941).
Wada Kiyoshi, *Shina Kan-Sei Hatten Shi* (Development of Government control in China), 1942; *Shina Chiho Jichi Hattatsu Shi* (Development of Local Autonomy), 1939.
Wang K'ao-t'ung, *Chung Kuo Shang-yeh Shih*, 1936 (Japanese translation by Sekino, 1940).

CHAPTER XVII

TRAITORS AND ALIENS: THE FALL OF THE SUNG AND THE MONGOL OCCUPATION

The Sung period saw an enormous increase in economic activity in China proper and the northern borderlands. People of various classes and groups were largely taken up with the pursuit of wealth and luxury for themselves. There was a great extension of the arts and graces of life, of comforts and pleasures in which all classes strove to increase their share. The limited value of the class-war theory may again be illustrated from this period. That theory is useful in helping to identify and define certain group-interests in a generalised way; but the more sharply it does so, and the more exclusively it insists on its own limited criteria, the more it distorts the picture of the real society.

In the class explanation, the Sung period appears as a great age for the 'big gentry'. Certainly, it was an age of great and increasing rural estates. Large-scale landowning flourished, to an extent even exceeding that of the T'ang period. This is, however, a judgment by results, rather than the identification of a causal factor. From this time onwards, landowning remained the chief criterion of social position, success or rank, in China. Commercial or industrial investments might often be more lucrative, and the opportunities for them were much increased, but they were generally regarded from a shorter-term point of view; the ultimate source of capital funds, as well as social prestige, was the land. The Sung gentry were men of varied kinds and origins. The proposition is rather that 'successful men became landowners' than 'the landowners became the victorious class'.

The view may indeed be taken that there was no dominant class, but rather a sustained equilibrium between the classes. Wealth, production, markets and the possibilities of personal consumption and enjoyment, increased all round in this period. Each class and group was concerned rather to make the most of all these possibilities, on a narrower basis of family and clan or clique relations, than to assert its own ascendancy in class terms. The age is one which produced no deep or systematic philosophies or political conceptions, but hundreds of lyrics, novels, amusements and the like; there are no highly coloured or forceful traits in its art, but a more subdued and generalised elegance, a broad appreciation of good living for its own sake. A non-committal attitude was generally the cultural preference.

These are not the characteristics, on the non-economic plane, of a new and rising class, asserting itself and its own view of life. On the economic plane, a very significant fact is the extent to which almost all functions or initiatives were given to the State. Able individuals, and coteries of individuals, took the administrative lead. Men rode the tide of economic expansion and enrichment, in a spirit mostly of opportunism, not with any preconceived social, patriotic or class-conscious aim. The general course of the economy was inflationary, to a high degree.

The standard identification of approximately this period as the beginning of Modern Times and the end of the Middle Ages, in China, has therefore some merit but serious disadvantages. (Some writers tend to place the turning-point in the succeeding Mongol period, which brought important changes in the international situation of China, and in the technical and administrative outlook; others, especially those who are eager to mark the first entry of the bourgeoisie, place it farther back in the T'ang period.) The merit of the view lies in drawing attention to the first emergence of features which have been only too characteristic of Chinese society in the much more recent period. The disadvantages lie chiefly in the implied analogies with Europe, fostered on the one hand by those idealists who wish to think of mankind as being of the same mind in all countries, and on the other by those who wish to reduce the history of all peoples to a common pattern, in order to bring them to a common end.

In Europe, at an equivalent stage, the middle classes were ready and able to assert their own distinctive conceptions and methods in every aspect of life, spiritual as well as material, from the highest conceptions of religion to the slightest details of commerce. The ground for the development of nationalism and class-consciousness was by then well prepared in the West. The same conditions only matured much later in China, in different and weaker forms, and in circumstances of great external pressure and internal confusion. The consolidation of the Sung period was succeeded by two very crushing periods of foreign domination, under the Mongols and the Manchus, which imposed a fairly thorough and prolonged subjection of Chinese initiatives. These ages of foreign rule and their aftermath did little to encourage the positive forces making for social development, in the direction of capitalism or any similar evolution, while tending to confirm and perpetuate the negative features in the older form of Chinese society.

* * *

An important aspect of the failure of the Sung is the great inflation which occurred in that period; a full study of this topic is much needed. The Sung greatly expanded not only the political frontiers of China, but also the dimensions of its economy and finance. The revenues of the State enormously increased from the start, especially the contribution of South China. Before long it was more than double that of the T'ang. But expenditure by the Government increased even more rapidly. The army was brought under the civilian authorities. This was apparently a wise measure, preventing the generals from taking local or central power, and bringing them on to the same basis as the other types of landlords or gentry. The generals were retired on pensions. Conscription was abandoned, and the ranks were filled with State-paid mercenaries.

The army soon began to increase again in numbers; but not so much as a fighting force, since the hired soldiers were put to work on the land, in depopulated districts or newly colonised areas. This was often like a State subsidy to landowners, who used these men as labourers or as peasant settlers. These landlords might be actually the officials in charge, or connected with them. Significantly, however, the soldier-labourers were able to resist exploitation to some extent—again, at the expense of the State. They constantly exacted more pay and allowance for less work. They refused, for instance, to carry their own baggage.

The Government followed in every case the line of least resistance. The neighbouring peoples in the North were bought off with tribute payment. The increasing use of money offered a ready means of raising funds. There was an enormous increase in the production of metals, and in the demand for coins, between the ninth and the eleventh century. For its high value, silver began to be preferred to copper as the material for coins; costs of transport and minting were relatively very high, and silver could bear these charges, while the cost of producing copper coins often amounted to their face value. There was much speculation in the different types of coinage, and in the deposit certificates issued by the State, which appeared at that time as the first form of paper money.

The tribute to the northern peoples (in the eleventh century, the Khitan Empire) was also paid in silver and coins, and horses were purchased from them in large numbers by the Sung. The Khitans (now called the Liao Dynasty), with their capital at Peking, became rich, and acquired much the same outlook and way of life as the Sung Chinese, in all matters, material and intellectual. They, too, were for a long time satisfied with the *status quo*, or the line of least resistance. They similarly maintained, by diplomacy and concessions, a balance of power, or a peaceful partnership, with their northern and north-western neighbours. Internally, they too improved their revenue system, and took the easy path of inflation. The inner fringe, at least, of the northern tribal areas became very much assimilated to Sung China, not only in the sense of racial fusion, but also of thus adopting the same type of economic system and general way of life. The only other state of importance in the eleventh century was the Western Hsia, in north-west China; this was a Tibetan country, in language and adherence, originally founded in the sixth century by survivors of the Toba, who joined with Tibetan and Tangut tribes in that area. Both Sung and Liao cultivated good relations with this State, and tried to keep it in the same balance of economic progress and inflationary prosperity that prevailed between themselves.

It was under such an opportunist policy as this that equilibrium was maintained between the 'Middle Kingdom' and its neighbours and unprofitable warfare largely avoided, while the whole area became more integrated economically than ever before, as a wide market area, currency area and trade network, in the course of one or two centuries of extensive development in which the inflationary stimulus and rising standards of consumption were widely shared.

Meanwhile, in China proper there was an important difference between the northern and southern parts of the country, which may help to explain why the North fell quickly before a new foreign invasion at the end of the dynasty, while the Southern Sung still resisted. The North never recovered fully from the war damage it suffered in the tenth century. Big-scale landownership was not so prevalent there, and cultivation depended largely on free peasants, or on tenants who were left a considerable degree of freedom under absentee landlords.

The officials, in both North and South, gradually got themselves (or rather their own lands) largely exempted from taxation. A heavy fixed tax was however levied on tenant holdings. The State revenues came to a disproportionate extent from the North, and from the tenant class. The settlers in the North were exploited and discontented, to the point of being ready to rebel. The Shensi area was attacked by the Western Hsia State, but in that case both the Sung and the Liao were willing to fight back for its possession.

It was inevitable that the corruption and self-interest of the officials should grow rapidly and enormously, in this period of inflation, opportunism and increasing trade opportunities. Official salaries had always been small; in this major inflation, they became insignificant, and simply had to be supplemented by other means. In the reign of Shen Tsung (1068–85), a definite stand was made against these tendencies, by the famous Wang An-shih. The Emperor, being concerned about the succession of budget deficits, was dissatisfied with the officials who advised him that things would right themselves, if only the dealers were left alone, when trade and revenue would increase. Wang An-shih gained the confidence of the Emperor, who approved schemes of reform, directed against the large monopolists and for the relief of the smaller farmers and tradesmen. Farm credits, price-stabilisation schemes, the 'ever-normal granary', the reduction of the army, the reform of civil service recruitment and pay-scales, and other measures were all included in the proposals. Wang An-shih was overthrown before these experiments could be taken very far; and the whole affair is so much bound up with political and other alignments and intrigues outside the economic sphere (including even literary disputes) that it needs to be studied very cautiously from the point of view of economic history. Wang An-shih's followers actually returned to power in 1102, but were again overthrown before they could implement their policies.

The downfall of the Sung was by then approaching. In 1114 a new military power appeared in the North, in the rear of the Khitans; the Jurchens (a Tungus tribe) declared their independence from the Khitans. They took Peking later, and destroyed the Liao Empire in 1125. On the Sung side, there was even some joy at the destruction of the Liao; but it was short-lived, as the Jurchen went straight on to capture the capital of the Sung in the following year. The Emperor's brother escaped to found the Southern Sung Dynasty, which lasted more than a century (1127–1279), with its capitals first in Nanking and then in Hangchow.

The Southern Sung had considerable resources in the southern part of the country. Their inclination was to continue the old policy, but at first they had to fight, because the Jurchen would not negotiate. The military party, under the leadership of Yo Fei, was well able to hold off the Jurchens, though not to defeat them completely. Yet the old policy prevailed; Yo Fei was assassinated by the party of Ch'in K'ui, representing the landowning interest, who was able to negotiate (1165) a state of near-peace with the Jurchens, on payment of a tribute, which was at any rate less than the cost of defence. The military party did regain power in 1204; it attacked the Jurchen, but failed disastrously, losing further large areas to the enemy.

Meanwhile a new and greater power had arisen in the North —the Mongol Empire. It defeated the Western Hsia and turned against the Jurchen. The Southern Sung made an alliance with the Mongols, who helped them to defeat the Jurchen; whereafter the Sung found themselves almost defenceless against the Mongols on their borders. The Mongols held all China from 1280 till 1368.

The final period of the Southern Sung saw all the main tendencies of its age carried to the greatest extremes. A close study of its economic history would be extremely valuable, from that point of view. The inflation was carried to 'wartime' extremes. The State—as was noticed in the preceding chapter—operated all sorts of schemes for revenue and welfare services. Another reformer, Chai Ssu-tao, who may be reckoned in the succession to Wang An-shih, made unsuccessful attempts at reform. A large foreign trade grew up in the southern parts, in the hands of a large and influential community of foreign merchants from Western Asia.

* * *

The rise of the Mongol Empire was quite a long process; even its conquest of China extended well over a century (in the thirteenth century the Mongols were also occupied in the west). The Mongols were extensively experienced in administration, technical matters, and politics or diplomacy, as well as in warfare. They were actually welcomed by some Chinese. These included especially the peasants in the North, who had again fared badly under the 'Chin Dynasty' established by the Jurchens, which tried to continue the policy of the Liao rulers, without having the latters' ability. Collaborators included also most of the landlords in the South; the Mongols removed the Southern landowners from political power, but left them their wealth and social position.

Previous changes of dynasty had usually brought, at least temporarily, some relief for the peasants. Under the Mongols, the free peasants in particular found their burdens increased. Many of them were dispossessed, set to work for the army, or had their lands (in the north) turned over to pasture for the Mongols' horses; others were drafted to forced labour, for the construction or maintenance of the new capital of Peking. The rest continued under their old masters, and had to support a class of new masters over and above the old; a very large number of Mongols, and their assistants and employees from all over Asia (and, like Marco Polo, even from Europe) were installed as a privileged class. The administration was thoroughly centralised in Peking. The Mongol rulers patronised the Buddhist and Taoist cults, and endowed them heavily. For all this, and for its vast military organisation, still more revenue was required, and even more taxes were levied, falling more heavily than ever on the diminished class of free Chinese farmers.

If anything like a Chinese merchant class had developed, the Mongol occupation seemed immediately designed to suppress it. Chinese were forbidden to learn Mongolian or other foreign languages. They played a part only in the trade with the Indo-China area. Elsewhere trade and other functions were under the Mongols' State-control. One race of people from the Mongol Empire played a large part, in foreign business particularly: the Uighurs.

Two opposing sets of circumstances are really involved. The similarity—in very general terms, of course—with the present-day situation is so striking that this is another subject which deserves fuller and more careful study than it has yet received. China under the Mongols was part of a great Eurasian Empire, ruled by a race whose heartland was in Central Asia, but quite cosmopolitan in its outlook, and most of all in its technique of production, organisation, communications and administration. It was quite ready to adopt and use methods and persons from anywhere in its vast sphere of influence, all across Asia and in Europe, in the service of the vast machine it had built up, primarily as a means to world-conquest.

Marco Polo has given the best-known and most vivid example (though there were others). Such persons must have furnished a great deal of 'technical assistance' to China, under the Mongols. Marco himself, as a 'foreign specialist', enjoyed his experiences as a special envoy, governor of a district, etc., and wrote vividly praising the efficiency and power of the Mongol Empire. The West has been perpetually impressed by his brilliant work of propaganda on behalf of the Khans of Eurasia. Clearly, administration, roads, architecture, civil engineering, traffic and many other matters were vastly improved in China in this period. And China was linked with a vast pan-Asian complex, which should have meant unprecedentedly large markets, or at least interchanges of materials and knowledge, such as would transform the scale and speed of its economic development.

From the internal point of view also some positive improvement must have resulted. Peace and order had returned, and a very effective administration served to pull the country together again as a large and coherent economic unit. For such general reasons, there must have been some relative improvement.

There is, however, much evidence to the contrary: conditions generally deteriorated, especially for the lower classes of Chinese, to a terrible degree. Any benefits from the improved connections went to the cities, and to the foreigners. The drain of coins out of China was probably greater than in any other period; there were many depreciations of the currency, and a great paper-money inflation. The move of the capital, the administration, and much of the industrial capacity to the North, served the strategic needs and other preferences of the conquerors, but it was uneconomic; the Sung had kept the capital near the economic centre of gravity of the country, the producing regions.

Chinese merchants and craftsmen were able to earn their livelihood, but for the most part depended on foreign masters. These people sometimes took the lead in the numerous rebellions, but for the most part they were peasant movements of mixed and sporadic kinds; characteristically they were of the Robin Hood type, they attacked the rich (both Chinese and foreigners) to give to the poor. In the 1350's, under Kuo and his successor Chu—the former a beggar's son, the latter a peasant—a wider policy was developed by the insurgents. They won the support of many thousands of labourers who had been conscripted for 'flood control' work. They became more fully organised; but they also ceased their depredations against the rich Chinese, and won them over to the revolution. Hitherto, the Chinese gentry, fearing for their own lives and property, had sided with the Mongol authorities.

In fact, the Chinese landed interest had borne the main cost and trouble of suppressing the 'bandits' on behalf of the Mongols; because the latter, in this crisis, proved to be entirely weak. Their soldiers could not, or would not, fight. There had been a good deal of fighting and training in the 1280's. That single decade saw the expedition against Japan, which was a costly failure; the war against Burma, another drain on the Chinese economy; and the conquest of Indo-China, which did open a new market for China. In 1292 there was an expedition to Java, which also yielded no great profit, at least to China or its people. Thereafter the Mongol garrisons in China seem to have deteriorated very rapidly.

As is well known, the Mongol Emperors themselves became very much 'sinified', adopting the Chinese language, culture and customs in large part. They remained, however, in Peking, on the fringe of their Chinese domain; and they quit even that capital every summer, to spend the hot season in more northern places, enjoying the camp life of their own people.

Mongols of less exalted rank remained in China usually on a 'garrison' or 'tour of duty' basis. They made remittances home, and usually preferred to retire there. This applies more strongly to the other Central Asians who served under the Mongols.

It is probable that the Mongols regarded China as a special extension or supplement to their main and central Empire. The loss of Peking (which fell to Chu in 1368, after he had taken first Nanking, then the whole of the South) was a severe but not a fatal blow to the Mongols, who retired into Mongolia and regrouped their forces.

The economic aspects of the Mongol occupation require much more extensive and systematic study than has yet been devoted to them. The study would be most suggestive in view of the position of China today.

CHAPTER XVIII

ANTECEDENTS OF THE MODERN PERIOD

The last chapter referred especially to the exploitation of China in the period of Mongol occupation, which lasted some ninety years (A.D. 1280–1368). One very powerful and enduring consequence of this, among the Chinese people at large, was a deeply instilled xenophobia. No nation, in all history perhaps, has ever been entirely free from anti-foreign feeling or prejudice; but it has existed in China in the last few centuries in a particularly sharp and explicit form. The Mongol domination is perhaps especially or originally to blame for this, to a large extent. Under it, the presence of the foreigner, and political subjection to him (or discrimination in his favour) came to be primarily associated with economic exploitation by him of the resources of China and the labour of the Chinese. It is noteworthy that all revolts against the Mongols stressed primarily economic rather than racial grievances.

Ever since then, this association between the foreign presence and economic exploitation—alongside, or even transcending in importance, the consciousness of political or cultural subordination—has continued to be a weighty factor in the Chinese outlook and in Chinese politics. Western communities, which have not been historically so long under foreign domination or pressure, and have not suffered so protractedly from bad governments of their own, can hardly appreciate the rootedness and continuity of the psychological reactions which spring from this.

The oppressive Mongols were succeeded by the purely Chinese or national dynasty of the Ming (1368–1644). There was much that was good under the Mings, but unfortunately they displayed also many bad characteristics. Moreover, they were constantly under external or foreign pressures, often so great as to give them hardly a fair chance.

The Mings were succeeded by a new foreign group, the Manchus, whose system of dynastic rule and racial or caste privilege, over the next two centuries, appeared no less burdensome and detestable than the Mongol system. The Manchus were perhaps more single-minded and thorough in their economic and social exploitation of China than the Mongols had been, since they were based exclusively on the area of China. Whereas to the Mongols, China had been but one province or dominion in a much wider and less static Empire; and to the end the Mongols sought military prowess rather than material wealth.

Then, before the Manchus had fully run their historical span, China was subjected to the new and overwhelming influence of the technical civilisation of the West. The Manchus were flagrantly incapable of defending either themselves as a group, or China as a whole, against the tides from the West. The new forces brought in from abroad, in the nineteenth and twentieth centuries, were far more powerful and revolutionary than anything the Chinese had yet experienced.

Meanwhile, the internal pressure increased overwhelmingly; it must always be borne in mind that the relative over-population and shortage of land in China dates essentially from the eighteenth century. The great rise in population dates only from that epoch, and until the latter part of the eighteenth century there was actually land to spare.

Yet, though the intensity of economic evolution, and the power of forces specifically economic, were thus vastly increased in the last five or six centuries, and especially in the last century, the reactions of the Chinese became less and less exclusively economic or materialistic; racial, cultural, political and social grounds of opposition came increasingly to be stressed. Whereas the rebellions against the Mongols had hinged so largely on economic grievances, especially the physical plight of the peasants and tenant farmers, the resistance against the Manchus and against Western Imperialism—while of course including the economic element and economic motives—acquired an increasingly variegated and enlightened complexion, until the present period.

The Mings stressed, as far as they could, the cultural identity and superiority of China. Against the Manchus, racial feeling developed strongly—much more strongly, it is interesting to note, than it had developed against the Mongols. The chief explanation may be that the Manchus were much more evidently a single ruling race; the Mongols had depended very largely on a heterogeneous following of people from other Central and West-Asian tribes and groups. Perhaps the Russians would now be well advised to use their Central Asian citizens, as far as possible, for the development of the Brother Republic in China—if they are sufficiently trusted and capable for that important task. The anti-Manchu feeling was naturally centred especially in the South of China. Were the reasons for this economic or cultural? This question, and the true nature of relations between the North and South of the country, in general, are neglected and important fields of study.

However, the racial feeling passed easily into a more constructive force: the consciousness of the quality of the Chinese civilisation or culture, and the aim of building it as a still stronger alternative to the foreign spirit. Important new ideas were also taken up; current studies significantly bring out the profound influence of Christianity, for instance in the T'aip'ing Movement. This was of course crude and distorted, and it fell later into decadence and came to an evil end; but there is no gainsaying the power, even among the lowest and most ignorant classes of the population, of thoughts or instincts of idealism, internationalism and desire for progress (spiritual as well as material) which were at the heart of this 'ideology'. Christian missions generally may have had more historical influence than has yet been realised; the fact is perhaps measurable from the zeal with which the Communists are now trying to suppress them. Western-style liberal education was surely an even greater influence and is now being no less frantically combated.

From the humanistic point of view, it is encouraging that the modern revival and reassertion of Chinese culture itself stressed particularly the universalistic and humanitarian outlook on which it is so vitally based, within which 'all in the four seas are brothers'. A great Reform Movement grew up, based on idealistic principles; there was a considerable and sincere movement of internationalism and intellectual generosity. It is impossible not to feel that Kang Yu-wei or Sun Yat-sen (for instance) were moved by impulses on a plane of thought almost too elevated for these times.

* * *

In other words, there have been at least two planes of thought on which opinion has moved in modern times in China, as in other countries. One is concrete, materialistic and selfish, the other abstract and idealistic. Economic history is naturally concerned with matters that contribute to the former rather than the latter. It can clarify a great deal, but still is essentially limited to one half of the question; it covers only the substructure, and does not give a judgment of the whole civilisation. The present Communist attempt to make economic or class criteria the sole canons of historical judgment, besides being intrinsically defective, means that the sordid and materialistic impulses are stressed anew. In particular the illiberal and anti-foreign impulses, referred to above as inherited from the experience of recent centuries, are deliberately revived and exaggerated by this policy.

The basic and original theory of Marxism—which is a materialistic determinism—is contradicted by the fact that as economic concerns became more pressing, in the modern period in China, men's thoughts turned not more but less towards solutions and explanations that were directly or crudely economic. The true 'dialectic' is not a clash between two hypothetical classes, but the permanent struggle between the better and the worse impulses in the hearts of men of all ranks and races, and even in the mind of the single individual. In this context also, it is accurate to use relative, not absolute terms: to say, the 'better' and 'worse' impulses, not the best and the worst.

To cover the gap between its rigid theory and the fluidity of the real-life situation, neo-Marxism, in China even more than elsewhere, has been concerned to generate the maximum of moral indignation and psychological antagonism, which are the most effective enemies of factual realism and logical thinking. A close study of the agrarian reform movements in the Liberated Country, anti-corruption drives, proceedings of

People's Courts, etc., shows how little they have appealed to interests essentially objective or economic, but have been staged to promote public indignation and vindictiveness. Foreigners and native class-enemies are not usually arraigned for offences primarily or solely economic; all kinds of atrocities and treacheries have to be attributed to them. In extreme cases, the show is not complete without the whole gamut of psychological display, from abject confession by the prisoners to the mob shouting 'Sha, Sha!' (Kill, Kill). Apart from this dependence on arousing moral indignation or spite, other forms of emotionalism are heavily relied on by the latter-day Marxism, which claims a monopoly of patriotism and civic conscience.

Meanwhile the effort is systematically and tenaciously maintained by the Communists, in the historical field especially, to stress exclusively the sordid and materialistic interpretation; there is every justification for supposing that the real and ultimate aim is to make this the exclusive dogma, and that the lip-service to ethical and libertarian standards is a mere tactic, in the longer view. Liberal, democratic and cultural fellow-travellers will be thrown aside when they cease to be useful.

The study of the available materials on the history of China in the more modern period has therefore to be approached with something more than the ordinary scientific degree of caution. Owing to the present political complication, it must even be approached with suspicion. Even the most general questions involve difficulties on this score. Take, for example, the conventional designation of the basic periods in Chinese history. Even if the demarcation of the whole of the last five or six centuries as the 'modern' period is not deliberately tendentious in this sense, it contributes in practice to the effect in question. It supports the view that this period was an historical continuum, in which the social and economic forces which are now present as the end-result, were operative from the very beginning, and were causal, ensuring that the course of evolution in the period would follow a given (and more or less predetermined) process; that the whole period represents one single and definite cycle of class-struggle.

An alternative interpretation, which must also be critically regarded, stresses the relative suddenness and power of the impact of the West in the nineteenth century, the overwhelming effect of which is represented as almost a break in the course of Chinese history; in this view there was something of a head-on clash between a given Chinese economy and civilisation and a newly arriving, rather thoroughly incompatible, Western economy and civilisation, in which the latter was largely the victor.

The basic thesis of the present work is that China must be viewed in terms of the interplay of a large number of forces. These have been extremely variegated and mutable. They may, however, usefully be considered in two main groups. One group has been termed 'internal', contributing to the building up of the historic individuality of China; an outlook largely authoritarian, yet socially democratic, but economically, politically and culturally self-centred. 'Insular', as only a great and remote continental country can be, this nation has always in large part had a sense of what has been called 'centrality' and 'metropolitanism'. Only occasionally, however, has this situation been static; the internal forces themselves, and the equilibrium between them, have varied exceedingly from age to age. Collective history is an overlap of inheritances, just as personal or family history is an overlap of successive generations. Nevertheless, though the ruling tendency from the 'internal' point of view has been centripetal, the component elements have been extremely diverse and changeful, and defy any rigid scheme of 'class' interpretation.

The other main group of forces has been termed 'external'. To some extent these were merely local or peripheral, on the borders of China proper (borders which fluctuated greatly from the economic and cultural points of view, as well as the political). In that case, or if they were relatively weaker than the internal forces, they were absorbed into the complex evolution of China proper. When the conditions were otherwise, when the external forces were not localised or marginal, and were relatively stronger than the internal forces, they were able correspondingly to affect or assimilate the latter, and exert a centrifugal influence in the development of China proper.

The balance of forces, the nature of the forces themselves, and the pace of these developments, all varied enormously from time to time. What makes Chinese history so distinctive in the whole record of world history may chiefly be the possibility, which it peculiarly had, of alternately obtruding its influence on the world outside, and withdrawing into its own physical and mental boundaries. No nation has ever so concisely and accurately named itself, to display its own basic characteristics, as have the Chinese people, who from very early times have called their land the 'Middle Country'.

* * *

The rebellion of the Chinese against the Mongols, which was finally successful in 1368, was led by Chu Yuan-chiang, who was a peasant leader and a former monk. Only at a late stage did his movement acquire any national or patriotic character; and when it did, this was largely due to the action of the Mongols, who responded by increasing the severity of their nationality laws, which discriminated against the Chinese. The success of the rebellion seems to have been due to the weakness and military decadence of the Mongols within China more than to the prowess of the Chinese. The Mongols withdrew to Central Asia, which was always the 'heartland' from their point of view, and struck back very powerfully at the Chinese. The two peoples were constantly in conflict, throughout the Ming period, in the area of Turkestan. Once again, expansion in this region was to prove a drain on the resources of China; the area was broken up into a number of small states, in a shifting balance between Chinese and Mongol power, and its economic importance to China was much less than it was in other periods.

Another foreign power, a new one, pressed on Ming China from a new direction—the east. This pressure also meant negative economic effects of the most direct kind: the destruction of cities, crops and communications, pillage and the exhaustion of military resources. The pressure in question was that of the Japanese pirates, the Wako. Bands of Japanese seafarers or military adventurers, made frequent, well organised, and often large-scale raids on the eastern and south-eastern coasts of China. These took the form, not of sustained occupation or invasion, but of swift and ruthless forays on ports and inland towns. 'Acquisition without production' has always been an important though subsidiary factor in economic history, especially in the early stages of the growth of nations. The incursions of the Wako signalised the rise of Japan as a national power, whose bolder spirits were not content to remain entirely within their own little islands; but certainly the stirring of this hornets' nest is also attributable to the Mongols, who had attacked the Island Empire, and broken the peace of its former isolation.

As early as 1388, the Chinese established a system of fortifications around their eastern coasts. But they were unable to cover this long front, and its extended line of communications, against these raiding tactics. They attempted to build a navy, but the Japanese were always able to intercept and destroy these efforts. Later, the Ming resorted to a 'scorched earth' policy, the extent of which is a measure of their desperation in face of this particular menace. Many coastal settlements and whole populations in the affected provinces were transferred inland, their territory left desolate.

In the latter part of the fifteenth century, the Japanese maritime activities diminished, owing to the outbreak of internal troubles in Japan; but they remained a nuisance and sometimes a menace, until the end of the Ming Dynasty, in fact till the Japanese themselves 'closed' their country completely from foreign intercourse in the early part of the seventeenth century. From the sixteenth century European sea-rovers, armed traders and merchant venturers also began to appear on the southern and eastern coasts of China, and in the South-Asian seas in which the Chinese were also interested; frequently they too were guilty of conduct more or less piratical, and often they met with a most hostile reception.

These external pressures being considered, it is not difficult to realise how deeply anti-foreign feelings obsessed the Chinese mind in this epoch and after it; and to what extent all foreign contacts must have been associated all the time with negative, and even directly destructive results. The Ming closed the frontiers of China against all comers, and looked down on all barbarians as being uncivilised and unruly, and no better than robbers. A tremendous effort was made by the Ming Dynasty to set up a truly Chinese civilisation and society, as a positive alternative. The establishment of neo-Confucianism as a State doctrine and a social code, associated particularly with the name of Wang Yang-ming (1472–1529), was a great step in that direction.

There was a great revival of arts, literature and craftsmanship, all in specifically Chinese modes of expression. The name chosen by the founder for his dynasty is itself psychologically revealing, in this connection: 'Ming' signifies 'brilliance' and also clarity. Plain, unmixed and luminous colours prevailed in their art, and their personal and household adornments. Clear, enlightened and straightforward rules were sought in their philosophy and administration. But the desire for brilliance was fatal in one respect at least; the Court and the upper classes sought to maintain a degree of luxury and display that the country could by no means afford. Presumably they could not contemplate being inferior in these respects to the ousted Mongols; but the latter drew on the resources of a vast pan-Asian Empire to sustain their pomp, while the Mings held only a reduced and harassed China. Nevertheless it seems clear that the principal explanation is that they thought it simply natural and automatic to enjoy great wealth, that they had no approximate idea of the size of the national income, and practically no idea of where it came from: so much, perhaps, for the interpretation of history which regards human destiny as controlled by cunning calculations of economic self-interest on the part of ruling classes.

At the beginning of the dynasty, in any case, the ruler's intentions seem to have been clear, honest and disinterested. Many rich men and nobles were obliged to remove themselves to the new capital at Nanking, and to give up much of their landed property in other parts of the country, which was redistributed to poor farmers. A new census of land-holdings was made, with more comprehensive and accurate lists of real owners and their incomes, to prevent evasion of taxes by the powerful classes or families. The Buddhist Church and its landed endowment was greatly reduced, by similar measures.

These measures, theoretically excellent as they might seem, appear to have failed badly in practice. A root cause may have been the extravagance already noted; while society generally was living beyond its income, corruption increased. Bribery and greed became prevalent, as never before. They affected particularly the increasing class of merchants, who most needed wealth and ostentation as the means of 'social climbing'; and the officials, who were relatively underpaid. The latter were of course chiefly responsible for enforcing the reform laws; the result was that the laws were indifferently and unequally enforced.

Recent writers have stressed that one district, in particular, largely escaped having to comply with the reform laws. Namely, the region of the Lower Yangtse and its delta. This rich agricultural and trading area, which was by that time well settled and beginning to be thoroughly developed, is accounted a 'key economic area'. Reliance on this area was, however, rather for military and political than economic reasons. The pressure of foreign forces in the north and south-east, and the removal of the capital to Nanking, made it the natural base at the time. An additional reason was, however, that this had been the first district to be liberated from the Mongols, and continued to give good support to the Ming Emperors, doing more than any other district in supporting the army, the attempts to create a navy, and the life of the Court.

Although there was an increase in trade, no considerable middle class or capitalistic interest could develop for some time to come; to speak of the emergence of a bourgeoisie is still an exaggeration. In fact, in the Ming period, legislation against merchants and all their activities was extremely oppressive, and made the emergence of such a social class practically impossible in that period.

Political and social life was highly centralised in the Court; there were numerous and complicated struggles between 'cliques'. The policy of the earlier Ming Emperors may be characterised as Machiavellian; they sought to secure their own power, first and foremost, and tried to set one clique against another. The shifts of policy, and the composition of the cliques themselves, do not fit in very clearly with any pattern of economic class interests. From the latter part of the fifteenth century especially, the Court was largely under the influence of eunuchs. There were various risings in the countryside, under oppositional cliques; and foreign pressures increased, from the Japanese who invaded Korea in 1592–8, from the Europeans, and finally from the Manchus, who secured their own area of Manchuria in 1618. Formosa was under the Spaniards and Dutch, in the early seventeenth century, and they were later replaced by the independent Koxinga. The Manchus overwhelmed China, in the middle of the seventeenth century. The next and final chapter will discuss the modern period, which may be dated from the Manchu era (1).

NOTES TO CHAPTER XVIII

(1) There is practically no literature bearing specifically on the ground covered in the above chapter. From the point of view of a student's reading course, the following may now be listed, in addition to the bibliographical references already given, as helpful in the characterisation of the modern period and its beginnings.

Aritaka Iwao, *Chukoku Shakai Shi*, 1948; and (better) *Gaikan Toyo Tsushi*, 1950.

Ch'en Teng-yuan, 1936 (Japanese translation by To-A Kenkyujo, same title, 1943).

Ch'ien Mu, 1940, 1948.

Chinese Communist Party, approved works: Hsu Li-ch'un, 1942 (Yenan period—patriotic, and respectful of Chinese traditions); *Symposium*, 1950. (Neo-orthodox. Economic aspects stressed, almost to *reductio ad absurdum*. Iconoclastic; striking contrast with last-mentioned work. Emperors called by their personal names, instead of dynastic titles.)

Eames, J. B., *The English in China*, 1600–1843. London, 1906.

Fitzgerald, C. P., *China, a Short Cultural History*. Revised ed., 1950.

Franke, O. *Die Rechtsverhältnisse am Grundeigentum in China*, Leipzig, 1930 (Japanese translation by Shimizu Kinjiro, Shina Tsuchi Seido Ron, 1941).

Goodrich, L. C., *Short History of the Chinese People*, 1943.

Grousset, R., *China and Central Asia* (English translation by C. A. Phillips), 1941.

Hirase Minokichi, *Kindai Shina Keizai Shi*, 1942.

Hozumi Fumio, *Shina Kahei Ko*, 1944.

Kato Shigeru, 'On the Manor', in *Toyo Gakuho*, x, 2, 1932.

Kotake Fumio, *Kindai Shina Keizai Shi Kenkyu*, 1942.

Ku Sui-lu, *Bankmässige Transaktionen im inneren chinesischen Verkehr*, Hamburg, 1926.

Kulp, D. H., *Country Life in South China*, 1925.
Kyoto University (symposium), *Shina Chiri Rekishi Taikei*, Hyakuyosha, 1941; *Shina Kinyu ni Kankei suru Juyo Bunken Mokuroku*, 2 vols., 1940.
Madjar, L., 'Die Oekonomie der Landwirtschaft in China', in *Unter dem Banner des Marxismus*, III, 1, 1929 (Japanese translation by Inoue, 1935, a very popular Marxist text in Japan).
Miyasaki Ichisada and others, 'The Development of Social and Economic History', in *Shakai Keizai Shigaku*, x, 11–12, 1941.
Moriya Mitsuo, *O-shi no Zoku Fu no Kenkyu* (Investigation of the Genealogy of the Wang family of Shansi), 1951.
Morohashi Tetsuji, *Shina no Kazoku Sei*, 1940.
Morse, H. B., *Chronicles of the East India Company trading to China, 1635–1834*, 5 vols., 1926–9.
Nakayama Hachiro, 'Latest Researches in Chinese Economic History', in *Hitsotsubashi Ronso*, XI, 3, 1943.
Shimizu Morimitsu, *Shina Shakai no Kenkyu*, 1939; *Shina Kazoku no Kozo*, 1942; 'Rural Administration in China', in *Shakai Koseishi Taikei*, 1949; *Chukoku Zokusan Seido*, 1950; *Chukoku Kyoson Shakai Ron*, 1951.
Steiger, G. N., *History of the Far East*, Boston, 1932.
Takekoshi Yosaburo, *Wako Ki*, 1940 (English translation by Watanabe Hideo, *The Story of the Wako*, 1940).
Tanaka Suiichiro, *Toho Kindai Shi*, 1943.
Williams, S. Wells, *The Middle Kingdom*, 2 vols., 1848; rev. ed., 1907.
Yano Jinichi, *Shina Kindai Shi*, 1940; *Kindai Shina Gaiko Shi*, 1930.

CHAPTER XIX

THE MANCHUS AND THE MODERNS

The last chapter discussed the Ming period, which lasted from the fourteenth to the seventeenth century, the very time of the Western world's transition from the medieval period to modern nationalism. It was noted that two powerful impulses were inherited from that phase of Chinese history. These were: a peculiar and acute form of xenophobia, and an intense desire to maintain and enjoy the traditions and values of the ancient and integral culture of China itself. The former reaction was understandable and justifiable, considering all that the Mongol domination had meant in exploitation or discrimination against the Chinese. This was bound to lead to a bitter and prejudiced anti-foreignism, which was continued and reinforced in the succeeding Manchu period (1644–1911).

Materially, the life of the Chinese may have been more prosperous and pleasant in times of foreign rule than in those of 'indigenous' dynasties. In the Mongol period, China benefited economically and technically from being part of a vast pan-Asian unity; while the first part of the Manchu period saw phenomenal progress through peaceful and orderly development. The studied comparison of actual standards and patterns of living, between different historical periods, is another important and neglected field of research.

In respect of the second feature, the desire to cherish and develop a specifically Chinese society and civilisation, the effort of the Ming may be called a glorious failure. Whatever the artistic and literary results, gross faults and evil consequences followed in economic life and government. These led to a state of affairs so bad that foreign domination may even have seemed a lesser evil.

One of the most characteristic actions of the Ming was to rebuild the Great Wall of China. Another was to build the city walls of Peking, and to complete many palaces which the Mongols had begun there. It is not easy to explain such developments in terms of the 'economic interests of the ruling class'.

Nearly all the descriptions of the contemporary emergence of a 'bourgeoisie' seem to be exaggerated. Critical opinion greatly developed, since the use of printing had so progressed as to make books widely available; the number of entrants for the State examinations greatly increased. Intellectually, a middle class was emerging in this sense; but socially, economically or politically it had no distinctive existence. The systems of Court life and princely patronage still set, as rigidly as ever, the conditions of personal advancement. In one region only were there even the beginnings of the type of economic class differentiation which is here in question: in the new, and now central, granary area of the Lower Yangtse. There was little or no industry, beyond the handicraft basis; an important exception is the pottery centre of Ching-teh-chen in Kiangsi, a case comparable in importance to those of contemporary great enterprises in Europe.

Economic patterns were subordinate, on almost every count, to aesthetic, social and military motives. From the economic point of view the early Ming was soundly based on the Yangtse area, with Nanking as capital. It seems to have been merely through a dynastic dispute, originally, that the Yung Lo Emperor (1403–24) transferred the capital to Peking. But the move was a victory for the military party; for strategic reasons the capital remained at Peking, at heavy cost to the economic interests of the regime and the country.

Internal and local trade was ruthlessly suppressed; foreign traders were hounded out of the country, or simply massacred. Chinese traders could continue only as suppliers to the Court or the lordly classes. In the second and third decades of the fifteenth century, the great canal system was extensively restored, for the (uneconomic) maintenance of the capital in the north. The sea route along the east coast was controlled by the Japanese.

In the Yung Lo period there occurred also an expansion into south-west China and Indo-China, and the famous overseas expeditions of Cheng Ho. The economic motives for these developments were surely slight. Imports could have been obtained much more easily and cheaply by allowing foreign merchants to continue coming to China. The south-west and Indo-China did represent an additional market; but this motive was evidently subordinate to the desire to pacify these areas, which were centres of continuous rebellion and resistance. Last, but not least, this was a strategic direction for building up Chinese sea-power and recovering lost military prestige.

Both domestic and foreign policy were subject to the struggle of cliques and factions. The Ming Government became ever more of a police State. Its policy was to set rival factions fiercely against each other, recking little of the social consequences, and still less of the economic effects. There were various risings in the sixteenth century; the Mongols and the Jurchen tribes pressed on China in the North, and the Japanese occupied Korea in the last decade of the century. At the beginning of the seventeenth century, the Jesuit missionaries made their way into the Chinese Court, the independent Koxinga dominated Formosa and the south-east coast, and European traders appeared on the south coast.

* * *

The victory of the Manchus, like the victory of the Mongols, may be ascribed rather to shortcomings on the Chinese side than to the essential superiority of the foreign conquerors. The Manchus in their homeland had already adopted Chinese ways. They were regarded rather as a new group of rebels, than as extraneous invaders. Their military system was, however, superior, and their morale much higher. The numerous rebellions and factional struggles in China in this period were remarkable for their bloodiness; the populations of great and rich provinces, like Shantung and Szechuan, were decimated.

Factions which gained power seemed to have no idea what to do with it. All was lost in corruption and inefficiency. In these circumstances, a handful of disciplined and determined Manchus were able easily to seize and hold the country. The gate was opened to them. One of the successful Chinese partisans, Li Tzu-ch'eng, overthrew the Ming and proclaimed himself Emperor—but did nothing to consolidate his power. A rival, Wu San-kuei, making an alliance with the Manchus against Li, drove him from Peking. Immediately, the Manchus took power in China, and Wu became their subordinate general.

The Manchus were brutal in their racial contempt for the Chinese. They imposed immediately such signs of subjection as the wearing of 'pigtails'. Intermarriage was prohibited. A curious dual system of administration was established, with a Manchu and a Chinese side by side in each office; the Manchu, always the senior, was there by appointment, while his Chinese colleague had to pass the Civil Service examinations. The Chinese were dispirited, and without national leadership. In all classes they were thoroughly indifferent, or disgusted with the Mings; most of all, however, the landlords and 'gentry'. In Central China, where they had originally been the main upholders of the Ming, these classes went over to the Manchus, after a while.

Generally speaking, the Chinese remained indifferent or neutral, in the first two decades of the Manchu epoch, between the new dynasty and the 'other rebels'. But soon the Manchu rule brought marked economic and social improvements. The Government was cleansed of corruption and intrigue. There was again full employment for the scholar class, in all posts, alongside the Manchus. Depopulated areas were resettled; the simple restoration of continued peace and order was sufficient (as it has been in most periods of Chinese history) to allow China to make significant cultural progress, and recover her material prosperity. The upper and lower classes of Chinese were alike under foreign domination and discipline, and in this situation the gentry were obliged to treat the peasants better. Recovery was very marked in the K'ang Hsi period (1663–1722). It continued for perhaps another half century, through the reigns of Shih Tsung (1723–36) and Ch'ien Lung (1736–96).

K'ang Hsi subdued the South, the South-west, and Formosa. These campaigns, based on the Yangtse granary area, did not impoverish the economy of China proper. The same may be said of the campaigns of Ch'ien Lung, who was able, with relatively small armies, to put Mongolia, Turkestan and Tibet into subordination, enlarging the Empire and gaining vast tribute, without corresponding outlay. Meanwhile, with internal peace and order, population and output rose enormously. The proceeds were largely invested in new buildings and urban improvements, especially in Peking, with the use of paid, rather than forced, labour—which caused a condition of 'construction boom' to prevail for some time.

Yet, towards the end of the eighteenth century, there was an increasing tendency towards decline and crisis. When, why and how this happened may be questions ultimately as important, from the point of view of world history, as the corresponding questions about the course and genesis of the French Revolution which occurred at about the same time. For the economic history of the period, some proper census figures and agricultural statistics are fortunately available. The statistics show that the cultivated area did not increase in proportion to the population. Agriculture became more intensive; it was in this period, historically, that Chinese agriculture first reached that extreme degree of intensiveness which is now its most essential characteristic, and that the density and distribution of population took something like their present forms.

Subsistence was at first well maintained, and a surplus available for governmental and other levies; but eventually the growth of population so changed the *per capita* calculation that living standards were significantly reduced. It was probably not feasible to import foodstuffs, and in any case such a policy was not considered. There was some growth of general trade. Banking had also developed, to some extent. It was, however, chiefly limited to the financing of spot business and cash trade: credit business, an investment system or the process of capital formation in the European senses of these terms, can hardly be said to emerge till a whole century later. Nor did any industrial development take place, comparable to what was already accomplished in Europe. In industry, the criteria and conditions continued to be those of craftsmanship.

The whole situation differed from that which, in Europe, had led first to the emergence of a middle class or bourgeoisie, in the industrial sector of society especially, and thence to the advance of that class to a position of social ascendancy. The gentry invested in land—as they have continued largely to do, right up to the present generation. From the point of view of the social system, they were concerned to keep artisans or tradesmen in subjection and dependence, and to maintain the agrarian and 'regulated' basis of society.

Certain industries developed. Some (porcelain, carpets, arms, etc.) were on a fairly large scale; and, as in Europe at the corresponding stage of history, these were primarily connected with Court and luxury demands on the one hand, and the needs of national defence on the other. But the gentry, right up to the breakdown of the Chinese system in the last days of the Manchu Dynasty, were concerned to prevent and obstruct the spread of anything like 'industrialisation', such as had already become the destiny of Europe.

By the beginning of the nineteenth century, the new phase of decline was therefore far advanced. It was not the pressure of the foreigners from the West, which then made itself fully felt, that brought the ruin of the Chinese society of the Manchu period; that ruin was already evident. The south-west was the only region open for Chinese immigration; its arable land area became fully settled during the eighteenth century. In the older settled regions, the power and wealth of the landowning classes declined (in comparison with preceding periods). If a 'modern' middle class was created in China in the early nineteenth century, the differentiation may or may not have been economic in nature. It was not functionally economic; for the people concerned were not yet free to find a new social role in industry or trade.

There was, however, a differentiation in their plane of living; while some continued to enjoy the positions of landowners and senior administrators, an element of 'poor scholars', impoverished gentry or 'petty gentry', and even a large stratum of declassed persons, a 'floating population' of intelligentsia or adventurers, came into prominence in a new way, distinct from the part played by any such elements in earlier historical times. It is worth noting that a comparable development occurred even earlier and more significantly in Japan, where similar social elements figured as 'Ronin'.

The first rebellion against the Manchus came in 1774 in Shantung; the next year the White Lotus Society led a fiercely Nationalistic and anti-Manchurian rising in Honan, which was only suppressed after twenty-five years of large-scale military operations and political persecutions. The Manchus were blamed for everything, including evils which had existed long before the Manchus appeared, and were inherent symptoms of the Chinese society itself—which the Manchus had by this time fully adopted. From this time onwards, opposition movements in China tended widely to focus all popular discontents and hatreds on the foreigners of all races. Another large-scale rising (of the T'ien Fa Society) troubled the whole of North China in 1813.

On the northern border commercial and diplomatic contacts with Russia date from the Treaty of Nerchinsk in 1689; forty years later, an office was set up in Peking for Mohammedan Affairs, with resident representatives of the Central Asian peoples. All these matters came under the Manchu Government's 'Board for Regulating Barbarians'. Contact with the British developed earlier than is generally realised. The British occupied Bengal in the 1760's; the Chinese conquered Burma in 1769, and Nepal in 1790. The Manchu campaigns to the north-westward must primarily have been intended to protect Manchuria and North China. Economically, these ventures were not strikingly profitable—though they do not seem to have meant a heavy loss, as in previous periods. The primary motive of their campaigns to the south-westward, as far as Indo-China, must similarly have been the protection of the Central China area; again, they involved economic advantage only as a limited and subordinate motive.

In the case of the expeditions as far afield as Burma and Nepal, however, no solid economic motive can have applied. Apart from the desire to punish disrespectful barbarians, the Manchus were well aware that the West Europeans were dividing South Asia between them, and must have intended to assert the counter-claims of China—claims which were re-asserted by the Nationalists quite recently.

Fortunately for the Manchus there was peace on their eastern flank, since the Japanese had adopted, at the end of the Ming period, a policy of complete National seclusion. But Western pressure soon developed in the south and south-east, with powerful effects. The reign of Tao Kuang (1821–50) marks a new period. Western influences then began to penetrate deep into Chinese life. European traders won a limited foothold for business at Canton and Macao, but they deeply influenced South China and all the coastal areas. This now became the theatre of operation of the 'external' forces working on China. The overlording dynasty in the North took a conservative stand, as representative of the ancient Chinese conceptions in general, and of the sense of centrality in particular, trying to rally the 'internal' forces of China on its side.

The Manchu rulers' method was to impose the medieval pattern of trade, social regulation and contempt of Barbarians. They set up a monopoly, under privileged Chinese merchants, the famous 'Co-Hong', which was an elaborate system of regulation—and eventually of corruption. The Europeans sought to buy principally silk and tea, some artistic luxuries, and odd commodities such as rhubarb. There was little market for the European industrial products in exchange; it could have been developed, but the Manchu policy was concerned to prevent this happening. Thus opium came in, as the means of balancing trade; it was already well known to the Chinese, and eagerly sought by them.

Radically opposed conceptions of international relations, of social progress, of economic development, of civilisation itself, were here in conflict. The intruding Westerners reciprocated the ludicrous contempt which the Chinese showed towards them; they knew that the official policy represented neither the needs of China, nor the wishes of the Chinese people themselves. They may well have considered themselves great revolutionaries and harbingers of progress, battering down the rotten stage-setting of feudal monopoly and antediluvianism, to clear the way for all forms of enlightenment—just as heartily as any present-day Communist enjoys these impulses.

A few small salvoes sufficed to bring down all the defences of 'official' China, and rout its forces in all directions; apparently 'popular' China, the merchant classes or the masses, grieved little thereat, but willingly accepted (in large part) the new course. The doom of the regime, centred on the North, was now sealed—though it fought a long delaying action. Politically and nationally, China reached a state of extreme prostration, and the foreign powers displayed a shocking greed, rushing upon the inert body. A complete partition of China between the Powers seemed to be impending. This was on general grounds a considerable cause of resentment, shame, and other strong feelings. But in the particular life of individuals, adjustment was not so difficult. Great new prospects of employment and trade developed. The basis of Chinese society was reaffirmed in new activities, of a 'middle class' type, with a new kind of stress on the family system, and on certain provincial, clan, or guild relationships.

Propaganda has been much concerned to depict the adverse economic factors. These were certainly great in the nineteenth century. The chronically and increasingly unfavourable balance of China's foreign trade, and the drain of silver out of the country, brought widespread impoverishment to the upper and lower classes. Between these a new middle class emerged to some extent, which profited, accumulated some capital, became Europeanised, and laid the foundations of a native capitalism. State finances, from the same cause, became ever more uncertain, with forced and increasing reliance on foreign loans—the conditions of which were onerous, since capital was not available from internal sources, and the lenders' risks were very great. But this new middle class was not so large or important, quantitatively or qualitatively, as is sometimes postulated. Nor was it so clearly differentiated; it was still conjoined with both the upper and the lower classes.

Nor were the motives (of the partial and relative class differentiation that did take place) predominantly economic. The new ideas of the West were thoroughly studied and absorbed. A new synthesis of ideas and outlooks developed to a considerable extent, while an entirely new Nationalism and patriotism grew up, embracing novel and positive ideas and forms of organisation. As was remarked in the last chapter, the thoughts and programmes of such men as K'ang Yu Wei or Sun Yat Sen, and many others, are something much wider and more enlightened than the reflection of any economic or class interest.

The T'aip'ing Rebellion (1848–52) has recently attracted much attention from scholars and politicians. The People's Government is concerned to represent it as a forerunner of the present Communist Revolution (1). In fact, it represented a great mixture of agrarian-reformist, Christian, mystical,

Western and traditional-Chinese ideas and methods. It is very striking that these had such a wide and deep influence on this truly mass-movement of the Chinese people. It was primarily on political grounds that the Western powers supported the Manchus against it. The internal degeneration and collapse of the T'aip'ing movement is not to be explained very far by economic factors, which were on the whole essentially in its favour.

The adverse nature of the economic position in the later nineteenth century seems to have been exaggerated, when we remember that a phenomenal increase in wealth and productivity did take place in many parts of China, well expressed by the hoary clichés about the barren rock being transformed into modern Hongkong, and the mud flat into pre-liberation Shanghai. Railways, ports, industries and the rest did arise. By the twentieth century the democratic Republic had emerged, also Chinese enterprises and governments which could bear comparison with the foreign institutions, and promised shortly to be capable of replacing them.

The history of the last fifty years is, however, intensely and abnormally complicated by external pressures and changes, unparalleled in previous Chinese experience; to such an extent that it must largely be set apart from the rest of the record. Foreign pressure was so extreme that China was unable to mature into the phase of capitalism.

The older 'internal' forces had their final fling in the war-lord period of the 1920's, when they effected practically a counter-revolution, and threw the country back into conditions of provincial division and military strife reminiscent of the end of the T'ang period, or others in earlier history. This was essentially the result of the First World War, when the Western powers turned their attention almost completely from China, and Japan intervened to weaken further the Central Government; and of the subsequent period, when the Powers' interests were divided, and their relation to China was generally negative, except for that of Japan, which exercised increasing pressure.

Japan's seizure of Manchuria was a decisive event, as a move against both China and Russia. It is a sobering thought that practically all of China's modern-industry capacity is in Manchuria, and was placed there mainly by the Japanese, within little more than a decade. Japan went further, however, to occupy practically all of northern, eastern, southern and central China, to drive the Chinese Government out into exile in the Far West; thus Japanese militarism was chiefly responsible for what was, from the historical perspective, a radical distortion of the natural economy of China.

Thus, Communism established itself in China in circumstances fundamentally artificial and abnormal. Even less than in the case of Russia was Communism here the result of normal historical evolution, and even more was it the fortuitous outcome of war, invasion, disaster and decay.

* * *

The internal and external forces are still at work, though perhaps in changing forms. China's future will shape itself to them, and not to the textbook systems, Marxist or other. The Marxist creed has already undergone fundamental changes, to explain how the dictatorship of the proletariat should be applied in a country without a proletariat, and to justify the national and imperialist purposes of Russia. It is not predictable what distortions this doctrine may not suffer in China, under conditions so different in time and place from those in which it was first formulated.

A clue to the future may be found in the economic features of modern China. The country was, from the middle of the nineteenth century, divided into four parts or zones, for all practical purposes. There were, first, the Treaty Ports and Concessions, where Chinese and foreign efforts and intentions joined in seeking and promoting the fusion of China with the capitalist and democratic world of the West. Second, there was South China, which had become much more progressive than the North, favouring a reasonable co-operation with the outside world. It is 'no accident', as the Marxists say, that the National Revolution originated in the South, and fell into difficulties when it moved north. The third, the North was at first relatively backward, economically and politically. When it did develop, it figured as an area under direct foreign control—first the control of Japan, now the control of Russia. In the fourth place, there was the hinterland of the provincial and peasant life—landlocked, agrarian China.

The Communists came to power in the last-named zone, whence they moved on to make the North their most important and strategic area. This preference is rigidly imposed by the strategic requirements of Russia. The South remains, so far, as a residual zone, where Communism is still doing battle with other ideas and interests. The internal forces are crystallising in a determination, united as never before, to secure the development and progress of China. The negative elements in the ancient Chinese heritage are being broken down, to such an extent that they can never emerge again, in anything like their old forms. The Communists cannot claim the credit for this result, which is due to a long evolution, in the perspective of which their own part appears very limited.

The external forces now pull China two ways, between the two great camps into which the world is frankly divided. Momentarily, the Chinese people on the mainland are allowed only to look to Russia for the economic and social development which they need. This is the quarter in which they are least likely—because of the facts of economic geography, because of all the antecedents of their cultural and social problem—to find what they need. Eventually China must turn again to the sunward side of the world for help and contact; then the brittle dogma of Marxism will crumble, and the party uniform, in which the past history of China is now being decked, will be contemptuously discarded by posterity.

Meanwhile, however, the actual evidence of history is being suppressed and falsified by the temporary masters of China; it is an urgent task to preserve the records. It is necessary also to maintain and extend our knowledge and understanding of China, against the day when the Communist Dynasty in its turn falls, and China is able to seek again for ideas from the free world (2), (3).

NOTES TO CHAPTER XIX

(1) BIBLIOGRAPHY, THE T'AIP'ING REBELLION:

Various authors, *T'aip'ing T'ien Kuo*, Peking, 1952.
Ch'eng Yen-sheng (compiler), Peiping, 1926.
Chien Yu-wen (Kan Yau-man), Shanghai, 1935.
Hamberg, T., *The Visions of Hung Sui-tsuan* (Hongkong, 1854) (Japanese translations by Aoki Tomitaro, 1942).
Hsiao I'san, Shanghai, 1933.
Kuo Ting-i, 1945.
Lo Yun and Yu Tsu-chi (ed.), Shanghai, 1931.
Meadows, T. T., *The Chinese and Their Rebellions*, London, 1856.
Naito Torajiro, 'Materials on the T'aip'ing', in *Shirin*, x, 3, 1926; reprinted with a bibliography, 1929.
Nashimoto Yuhei, *Taipin Tengoku Kakumei*, 1942.
Nohara Shiro, 'The Rice-tribute system of the T'aip'ing Kingdom', in *Rekishi Kenkyu*, I, 5, 1933.
Old Palace Museum, Peking, 1933.
Teng Yen-lin, Peking, 1935.
Toriyama Kiichi, 'The Real Nature of the T'aip'ing Rebellion', in Keijo (Seoul) University's *Toho Bunka Shi Soko*, I, 1935.
Toyama Gunji, *Taipin Tengoku to Shanghai*, Kyoto, 1947.
Wilson, A., *The Ever-Victorious Army: history of the . . . suppression of the T'aip'ing Rebellion*, Edinburgh, 1868.

(2) GENERAL BIBLIOGRAPHY, CHAPTER XIX

Anderson, A. M., *Humanity and Labour in China*, 1928.
Asakawa, K., *The Russo-Japanese Conflict*, 1904.
Bau Ming-chien, *Modern Democracy in China*, 1922.
Bell, C. E., *Tibet, Past and Present*, 1924.
Beresford, C. W. D., *The Break-up of China*, 1899.
Bernard, W. D., *Voyage of the 'Nemesis'*, 1844.
Bland, J. O. P., *China, Japan and Korea*, 1921; *Li Hung-chang*, 1917.
Borg, D., *American Policy and the Chinese Revolution*, 1947.
Brown, A. J., *The Chinese Revolution*, 1912.
Buck, J. Lossing, *Chinese Farm Economy*, 1930 (Japanese translation by To-A Keizai Chosakyoku, 1937); *Land Utilisation in China*, 1937 (Japanese translation by Miwa Takashi, 1938).
Burgess, J. S., *Guilds of Peking*, 1928 (Japanese translation by Shen Chen-chun, 1942).
Cameron, M. E., *The Reform Movement in China, 1898–1912*, Shanghai, 1931.
Chapman, O., *The Chinese Revolution, 1926–7*, London, 1928.
Cheng Yu-k'uei, *Chinese Maritime Customs, etc.* (Japanese translation by Kabayama, as *Shina Kokusai Shukyu Ronso* (China's International Balance of Payments), 1942).

Chu Ao-shian, *Le Régime des Capitulations*, 1915.
Clyde, P. H., *History of the Modern and Contemporary Far East*, 1937; *International Rivalries in Manchuria, 1689–1912* (Ohio 1928) (Japanese translation by Ueda Hayao, 1935).
Collins, W. F., *Mineral Enterprise in China*, 1918.
Clark, G., *Foreign Economic Rivalries in China*, 1932.
Condliffe, J. B., 'Industrial Development in the Far East', *C.S.P.S.R.*, XII, 1934; *China Today—Economic*, 1932.
Coolidge, M. R., *Chinese Immigration*, 1909.
Cordier, H., *Expéditions de Chine 1857–8*, 1860 (Paris, 1905–6).
Cressey, G. B., *China's Geographic Foundations*, 1933 (Japanese translation by Miyoshi Takezo, 1939); *Asia's Lands and Peoples*, new ed., 1951.
Davis, Sir J. F., *China during the War*, 1852.
Dugdale, E. T. S. (translation), *German Diplomatic Documents, 1871–1914*, reprinted 1940.
Fong, H. D., *Extent and Effects of Industrialisation in China*, 1929; with Franklin Ho, *China's Industrialisation*, 1931; various monographs, Nankai University, 1929–32 (Japanese translations by Arisawa Hiromi, as *Shina Kogyo Ron*, 1936, and Okazaki Saburo, as *Shina Kogyo Soshiki Ron*, 1939).
Gamble, S. B., *Peking, a Social Survey*, 1921; *How Chinese Families live in Peking*, 1933.
Gavit, T. P., *Opium*, 1925.
Golder, F. A., *Russian Expansion on the Pacific 1641–1850* (Cleveland, 1914).
Greenberg, M., *British Trade and the Opening of China*, 1952.
Harlet, G. E. P., *China Treaties*, 2 vols., 1908.
Hsiao I-san, 1927.
Hudson, G. F., *The Far East in World Politics*, 1937.
Hunter, W. C., *The Fan Quai in China*, Shanghai, 1882; *Bits of old China*, 1911.
Koh, T. F., *Silver at Work*, Shanghai, 1935.
Kohn, H., *History of Nationalism in the Far East*, 1929.
Kuo, C. P., *A Critical Study of the First Anglo-Chinese War*, Shanghai, 1935.
Laboulaye, C., *Les Chemins de fer en Chine*, 1911.
Lane-Poole, S., *Life of Sir Harry Parks*, 2 vols., 1894.
Latourette, K. S., *History of Early Relations between the U.S. and China, 1784–1844* (New Haven, 1917).
Li Chao-lo (ed.), 3 vols., 1831 (modern edition by Lo Chen-yu, 1925).
Liang Chai-pin, Shanghai, 1937.
Loch, H. B., *Personal Narrative of Lord Elgin's Second Embassy, 1860* (London, 1900).
Loch, G. G., *Closing Events of the Campaign in China* (London, 1843).

Macmurray, J. V. A., *Treaties and Agreements with and concerning China, 1894–1919* (2 vols., N.Y., 1921); contd. in Carnegie Endowment publication, *Treaties . . . etc., 1919–29* (Washington, 1929).
Macnair, H. F., *The Chinese Abroad*, Shanghai, 1924; *China in Revolution*, 1931.
Matsuda Tomoo, *Igirisu Shihon to Toyo*, 1951.
Mayer, W. F., *Treaties between the Empire of China and Foreign Powers*, Shanghai, 1906.
Meng, T. P., and Gamble, S. B., 'Prices, Wages and Standard of Living in Peking, 1900–24', in *C.S.P.S.R.*, x, 1926.
Michie, A., *Englishmen in China during the Victorian Era*, Edinburgh, 1900.
Milburn, W., *Oriental Commerce*, London, 1813.
Miyazaki Masayoshi, *Kindai Ro-Shi Kankei no Kenkyu*, Dairen, 1923.
Momose Hiroshi and Numada Tomoo, *Kindai Shina to Igirisu*, 1940.
Montalto de Jesus, *Historic Shanghai; Historic Macao*, Shanghai, 1909.
Morse, H. B., *The Gilds of China* (London, 1909); *International Relations of the Chinese Empire*, 3 vols., 1910–18; with H. F. Macnair, *Far Eastern International Relations*, Boston, 1931.
Muramatsu Yuji, *Chukoku Keizai no Shakai Seido*, 1949.
Naito Torajiro, *Shin Cho Tsushi Ron*, 1944.
Odell, S., *Cotton Goods in China*, Washington, 1915.
Oliphant, L., *Narrative of Earl of Elgin's Mission*, Edinburgh, 1860.
Pelcovits, N. A., *Old China Hands*, 1948.
Pott, F. L. Hawks, *Short History of Shanghai*, 1921 (Japanese translation by Hijikata, 1940).
Pritchard, E. H., *Crucial Years of Early Anglo-Chinese Relations, 1750–1800* (Washington, 1936).
Sano Gaku, *Shin Cho Shakai Shi*, 1931.
Shanghai Municipal Bureau of Social Affairs, *Cost of Living Index, 1926–31*, 1932; *Industrial Reports*, 1929–32.
Toyama Gunji, 'Shanghai Petty Trade', in *Toyo Shi Kenkyu*, I, 4, 1936.
U.S.S.R. (official publication, Central Executive Committee), *International Relations in the Epoch of Imperialism*, 9 vols., Berlin, 1931.
Vladimir, W., *Russia on the Pacific and the Siberian Railway* (London, 1899).
Wada Kiyoshi, 'Remarks on the Ching Dynasty', in *To-A Shi Ronso*, 1942.
Wolseley, G. J., *Narrative of the War of* 1860 (London, 1862).
Yano Jinichi, *Ahen Senso to Hongkong*, Kyoto, 1939; *Aro Senso to En-mei-en* (The 'Arrow' War and Yuan Ming-yuan), Tokyo, 1939.

(3) ADDITIONAL BIBLIOGRAPHY

(A) Periodicals in European Languages

Asia Major (pre-war series, Leipzig; post-war, London).
Bulletin of the Museum of Far Eastern Antiquities, Stockholm.

Chinese Social and Political Science Review (*C.S.P.S.R.*).
Harvard Journal of Asiatic Studies.
Far Eastern Quarterly.
Journal Asiatique, Paris.
Journal of the American Oriental Society, New Haven.
Journal of the Royal Asiatic Society (*ibid.*, China Branch, Shanghai).
Mitteilungen des Seminars für orientalische Sprachen an der Friedrich-Wilhelms Universität, Berlin.
T'oung Pao, Leyden.

JAPANESE PERIODICALS

Chukoku Kenkyu (Gendai Chukoku Gakkai, Tokyo).
Chukoku Kenkyusho: Shiryo Geppo; Shoho; Chukoku Hyoron; Chukoku Kenkyu.
Hitotsubashi Ronso, Tokyo.
Jimbun Gakuho, Kyoto (To-A Jimbun Gakuho).
Orientalica (Tokyo University, Toyo Shi Gakkai).
Rekishigaku Kenkyu, Tokyo.
Shakai Keizai Shigaku, Tokyo.
Shicho (Otsuka Historical Association, Tokyo).
Shigaku Zasshi, Tokyo.
Shinagaku.
Shina Kenkyu (Tokyo, Dairen, Shanghai).
Shirin (*Shigaku Kenkyukai*, Tokyo, Kyoto).
To-A Keizai Kenkyu (*Yamaguchi Kosho*, Kobe).
To-A Kenkyu Gakuho.
Toho Gakuho (*Toho Bunka Gakuin*, Tokyo).
Toho Gakuho, Kyoto.
Toho Bunka (Tokyo University Toyogakkai).
Toyo Bunka Kenkyu.
Toyo Shi Kenkyu, Kyoto.

(B) Works of reference

Aoyama Sadao, *Shina Reki Dai Chi Mei Yoran* (Tohobunka Gakuin, 1939).
Bolshaya Sovietskaya Entsyklopedia, see Chapter X, note (4).
Central China Institute (Nanking), *Zenkoku Keizai I-inkai Kankobutsu Mokuroku*, 1939; *Shina Keizai Zaisei Kinyu Kankei Shiryo Mokuroku*, 1939; *Shina Kancho Gyosei Hokorui Mokuroku*, 1940; *Shinabun Zasshi Naiyo Sakuin Mokuroku*, 1940; *Kabun Zasshi Kobo Mokuroku*, *Fuka Shimbun Mokuroku*, 1940.
Chang Heng (ed.), 1894. (The Japanese chronologies are better, see under Heibonsha, below.)
Charles and Powell, *International Index to Periodicals*, N.Y., 1948.
Chiang T'ing-hsi and others (comp.), the largest Chinese encyclopaedia: see the section 'Shih Huo Tien'.

Chu Shih-chia (comp.), 1934. (The 'gazetteers' are a most important source for this subject.)

Commercial Press, Shanghai, see Chapter VII, note (2).

Cordier, H., see Chapter VII, note (12).

Gardner, C. S., see Chapter V, note (9).

Harvard-Yenching, 1940, 1933, 1940.

Harvard-Yenching Institute, 1938 (the best modern dictionary for this subject, invalidating older work. Remarkable for ease of reference).

Heibonsha, *Toyo Rekishi Daijiten*, 1937–9.

Higashikawa and others, sections of *Shina Hosei Daijiten*, 1930.

Keizai Daijisho (Dobunkwan, 1917).

Kokusai Bunka Shinkokai, *Guide to Japanese Studies*, 1937.

Kyoto University, Economics Dept.:

Shina Kogyo (Mining) *ni kakawaru juyo Bunken Mokuroku*, 1940.

Shina Nogyo (Agriculture) *ni kakawaru juyo Bunken Mokuroku*, 1940.

Shina Shogyo (Commerce) *ni kakawaru juyo Bunken Mokuroku*, 1940.

Lin Mou-sheng, *Guide to Leading Chinese Periodicals*, N.Y., 1936.

Liu Ta-po, 1933 (the *2,000-year Historical Tables* is better in this class, but does not go back into the B.C. period).

Okamoto Ichiro, *Shina Shakai Keizai Daijiten*, 1944.

Osaka University of Commerce, *Keizai Gaku Jiten*, 1929.

Otsuka Shigaku Kai, *Toyo Shi Ronbun Yomoku*, 1936.

Peiping Library, 1929–36.

Shina Chiri Taikei, 1940–1.

Skachkov, see Chapter V, note (9).

Standard Translations of Foreign Names, 1934.

South Manchuria Railway, Dairen, *List of Publications*, 1941; *List of Materials*, 1944; *Classified List of Publications*, 1944; *Dairen Library List* (undated).

To-A Kenkyusho; To-A Kankei Tokeishi (statistical material) *Mokuroku*, 1942; *Rekkoku Tai-Shi Seiryoku Shinto Shi Bungei Mokuroku* (penetration of the Powers into China), 1942; *Rekkoku Tai-shi Toshi* (investment) *oyobi Shina Kokusai Shushi* (balance of payments) *ni kakawaru Bungei Mokuroku*, 1942.

Uchida Tomoo (ed.), *Shina Koyu Meishi* (proper names) *Jiten*, 1942.

Wang Chung-yu, *Bibliography of the Mineral Wealth and Geology of China*, London, 1912.

Weng Wen-hao (ed.), 1934. (The Kyoto Institute for Humanistic Studies recently made a reproduction on 1 : 4,000,000 scale (Albers Projection). On the other hand, a simplified small-scale version is widely available.)

Yauchi Wataru (ed.), Wada Kiyoshi (revised), *Toyo Toku shi Chiri Zu*, 1941.

APPENDIX.
CHINESE REFERENCES.

CHAPTER II.

(1) 王毓銓，

(2) 陶希聖，「中國古代社會之史的分析」一九二九年，「中國社會與中國革命」一九二九年。

(3) 郭沫若，「中國古代社會研究」一九二九年。

(4)「西漢經濟史」「史地叢」一九三一年。

(5)「食貨半月刊」。

(6) 馬乘風，「中國經濟史」。

(7) 呂振羽，「殷周代的中國社會」一九三五年。

(8) 曾謇，「中國古代社會」(上)，「中國社會史叢書」五，一九三五年。

(9) 陳嘯江，「西漢社會經濟研究」(中國社會史叢，一九三六年)。

(24) 冀朝鼎，

(28) 徐中舒，「古代灌溉工程起原考」中央研究院歷史語集五，二：一九三五年。

(29) 翁文灝，「古代灌溉工程發展史之一解」。

(30) 曾謇，「中國古代社會」(中國社會史叢書)五，一九三五年。

CHAPTER III.

(2) 古史辨。
(3) 顧頡剛，「禹貢半月刋」。
(4) 萬國鼎，「中國田制史」。一九三四年。鄭肇經，「中國水利史」，一九三七年。

CHAPTER IV.

(1) 五經。易經，書經，詩經，禮記，春秋。
(2) 四書。論語，大學，中庸，孟子。
(3) 管仲，管子。
(4) 墨子，老子，荀子，韓非子，司馬遷，史記。
(5) 劉逢祿，「左氏春秋考證」，一八二九年，「皇清經解」本。一九三三年。康有為，「新學偽經考」，一八九四年(一九三一年)。
崔適，「史記探源」一九一〇年，崔述，「考信錄」一九〇四年。
(8) 洪業，「春秋經傳引得序」一九三七年。
(9) 錢穆，「周官著作時代考」一九三二年。
郭沫若，「周官質疑」，(金文叢考)一九三二年。
(10)錢穆，「先秦諸子……」，大學叢書，一九三五年「諸子叢考」，「古史辨」四，六，一九三三至三八羅根澤，「管子探源」一九三一年。黃漢，「管子為戰國時代作品考」，一九三五年。
(12)容肇祖，「商君書考證」 一九三四年。
(15)「中國考古報告集」一九三四年。
(16)梁思永，
(17)吳金鼎。

CHAPTER V.

(1) 羅振玉，「殷虛書契」，一九一二年，一九一六年，一九三三年；「殷商貞卜文字」，一九一〇年；(流沙墜簡) 一九一四年•

(2) 王國維，「古史新證」一九二七年○「殷卜辭中所見先公先王考」觀堂集林，一九四七年○

(3) 董作賓，「甲骨年表」；「甲骨文斷代研究例」一九三四年，五等爵在殷商)中央研究院集刊，六，三，一九三六年•

(4) 郭沫若，「卜辭通纂」一九三三年；孫海波，「甲骨文編」一九三四年○

(5) 王國維，吳大徵，「說文古籀補」一九一一年○吳其昌，「甲骨金文中的殷代農稼情况」一九三十年；(金曆朔疏證 一九三六年•郭沫若，「两周金辭大系圖錄考釋」一九三五年。

(6) 容庚「金石書錄目」一九三六年；(歷史語言專刊)一九三一年；(金文編)一九三八年；(商周彝器通考)一九四一年•

(7) 徐中舒，「清華國學論叢」一，一(一九二七年)傅斯年，「周頌說」，「歷史語言……集刊」•
胡適，「說儒」四，三，一九三四年• 陳夢家，「古文字中文商周祭紀」一九三四年•揚寬「古代辨」七，一，一九四一年•

CHAPTER VI.

(3) 馮家昇・

(9) 梁啓超，「清代學術概論」，「飲冰室文集（中）」，一九三六年；「中國歷史研究法」一九三三年；穆錢，「中國近三百年學術史」一九三七年・

(12) 耒報考，一九三〇年、

CHAPTER VII.

(1) 齊思和，「燕京學報」，二八，一九四〇年・
胡厚宣，北大：「史學論叢」 一，一九三四年・

(3) 丁文江・

(5) 貢，助，徹・吳昌其・高耘暉・
河漢，二，五，一九三五年・

(8) 陶希聖，「辯士與游俠」，一九三一年。

(9) 唐慶增，「中國經濟思想史」一九三六年・

(10) 鍾風年。

(11)「四庫全書總目」，「四庫全書簡明目錄」・

(13) 東方學術協會編：「中國史學入門」一九四七年・
周予同，「學林」，一九四一年・

CHAPTER VIII.

(1) 司馬遷，「史記」. 班固，「漢書」. 范曄，「後漢書」。
(2) 梁玉繩，「史記志疑」。
崔適，「史記探源」。
王念孫，「漢書雜志」。
錢大昭，「漢書辨疑」.
周壽昌，「漢書注校補」.
惠棟，「後漢書補注」，「後漢書注補正」.
王先謙，「漢書補注」.
(6) 「太史公行年考」（觀堂集林）李奎耀「史記决疑」
(7) 荀悅，「前漢記」.
袁宏，「後漢記」.
王益之，「西漢年紀」.
(8) 徐天麟，「西漢會要」，「東漢會要」.
王應麟，「漢制攷」.
孫星衍，「漢官七種」.
程樹德，「漢律考」.
(9) 王昶，「金石萃編」. 容庚.
(10) 羅振玉，王國維，「流沙墜簡……」一九一四年，「學術叢編」一九一六年.
(12) 封泥；官印.「齊魯封泥集存」一九三一年. 徐堅，「西京職官印錄」. 瞿中溶，「集古官印攷」.
(13) 賈誼，「新書」。桓寬，「鹽鐵論」，王充，「論衡」
嚴可均，「全上古……」.「玉函山房輯佚書」.
盧文弨，張敦仁，王先謙，徐德培。
(14) 馬非百。
(15) 史海念。
(16) 劉道元。
(17) 鞠清遠，楊聯陞.

CHAPTER IX.

(3) 三老，考弟，力田。　李于魁，瞿昭族。
(5) 孫毓棠，賀昌群。
(7) 朱希祖，張純明。
(8) 楊聯陞，楊中一，陳嘯江，曾謇，許宏杰，汜勝
(10) 韓克信，湯曉非。「說文月刊」三，二至三。
(11) 吳景超。
(12) 宋毅貞，「王莽」。
(13) 陶元珍。

CHAPTER X.

(5) 瞿同祖，「中國封建社會」一九三七年。鄧之誠，
「中華二千年史」一九三四年。
(10) 奴婢，僮隸，佃戶。

CHAPTER XI.

(4) 武仙卿，「魏晉南北朝經濟史」。
(11)「帝邑攷」。
(12) 土斷。

CHAPTER XII.

(2) 屯田。
(4) 三長制。
(12)「齊民要術」。
(17)「課」。
(19) 中男，丁男。

CHAPTER XIV.

(2) 鞠清遠，「唐代經濟史」。
(3) 「……財政史」，「官營工業」一九三四年。

CHAPTER XVIII.

(1) 陳恭祿，「中國史」一，一九四〇；「中國近代史」一九三五。
陳登元，「中國田賦史」一九三六年；「中國土地制度」一九三一。
錢穆，「國史大綱」一九四〇年；「中國文化史導論」一九四八年。
許立群，「中國史話」一九四二年，(中國歷史研究會)，「中國通史簡編」，一九五〇年。
郭沫若，「十批判書」一九四六年。陶希聖，「中國政治思想史」一九三五年。

CHAPTER XIX.

(1) 「太平天國」一九五二年。程演生編 「太平天國史料」一九二六年。
蕭一山，「太平天國叢書」一九三三年。
「太平天國雜編記」一九三五年。
郭廷以 「太平天國史事日誌」一九四五年。
羅邕，尤祖蓋編：「太平天國詩文鈔」一九三一年
故宮博物館編：「太平天國文書」一九三三年。
鄧衍林，「關方太平天國史料史籍集目」圖書館學季刊，九，一，一九三五。
(2) 鄭友揆，「社會科學雜誌」。「清代通史」一九二七年。李光洛編：「紀元編」(一八三一年(新編)，一九二五年)。梁嘉彬，「廣東十三行考」一九三七年。

(3) 「中國經濟」，澤大研究會，南京。
「輔仁學誌」。
「新思潮」上海。
「古史辯」。
「食貨半月刊」。
「史學年報」。
「清華學報」。
「動力」上海。
「圖書季刊」。
「讀書雜誌」上海。
「燕京學報」（年報）。
「禹貢半月刊」。
張樌，「歐亞紀元年表」一八九四年。
陳慶其，「中國大事年表」一九三四年。
陳垣，「二千年朔閏表」一九二五年；「中西回史日曆」一九二六年。
蔣廷錫編：「古今圖書集成」。
「中國人名辭典」一九二一年；「中國古今地名大辭典」一九三一年。
「食貨志十五種綜合引得」一九三八年；「九通分類總纂」。
燕京學社：（一百七十五種日本期刊中東方學論文篇目引得）一九四三年；（日本期刊三十八種東方學文論目附引得）一九三三，一九四三年。
梁啓雄，（二十四史傳目引得）一九三六年，（二十五史人名索引）一九三五年。
劉大白，（五十世紀中國歷表）一九三六年；（二千年史日對照表）。
（國學論文索引）一九二九至　六　。
平心編：「生活全國總書目」一九三五年．（十通索引）一九三七年。
（標準漢譯外國人名地名表）一九三四年。
翁文灝編：（中華民國新地圖）一九三四年．（中國分省地圖）。

INDEX

For Product Safety Concerns and Information please contact our EU representative GPSR@taylorandfrancis.com Taylor & Francis Verlag GmbH, Kaufingerstraße 24, 80331 München, Germany